NICE IS

NOT

A
BISCUIT

PETER MEAD

DUCKWORTH

For my wife Sam, and my
sons Billy, Ben and Harry

First published in 2022 by Duckworth,
an imprint of Duckworth Books Ltd

1 Golden Court,
Richmond,
TW9 1EU,
United Kingdom
www.duckworthbooks.co.uk

For bulk and special sales please contact
info@duckworthbooks.com

Design and typesetting by Danny Lyle.

Printed and bound in the UK by Clays.

Print ISBN: 9780715654262
Ebook ISBN: 9780715654651

Contents

2 Stepping Stones 29

3 Management 55

| 4 | **Leadership** | **105** |

5 Strategy 133

Preface

I embarked upon this book before Covid-19 disrupted the rhythm of business life catastrophically and caused many businesses to close and jobs to be lost. The agency I founded was not immune to these market forces.

Working lives have been disrupted in an unprecedented way and businesses are faced with challenges the like of which they have never experienced before. Accommodating those people who want to work from home, as well as those who are desperate to get back to an office-based structure is going to be the challenge of the next decade.

It is more apparent than ever before that companies who create a culture which gives their employees something to believe in and gather strength from are going to be much better placed to face the uncertainty of the next few years.

Introduction:
Thoughts to Build a Business On

When we started Abbott Mead Vickers advertising agency in 1973, there were three quotes we tried to live by. The first is from the patriarch of the Rockefeller dynasty, who said:

> 'The ability to get along with people is a commodity like any other. The only difference is that I'll pay more for that commodity than anything else I purchase.'

The second is from Bill Bernbach, founder of DDB and probably the most famous advertising man of all time:

> 'I want a business full of nice and talented people. If they're nice but not talented there is no room for them but equally importantly, if not more so, if they are talented but not nice I don't want them around either.'

The third is from Bobby Kennedy with, I think, apologies to George Bernard Shaw:

> 'Most people see things as they are and ask why? I dream of things as they could be and ask why not?'

Not a bad trio of quotes to guide you through your business life.

Abbott Mead Vickers' success was made possible first of all because in David Abbott and Adrian Vickers I stumbled across two truly like-minded partners. The combination of our bond of friendship and respect and our shared convictions about the way a business should evolve enabled us to shape AMV into the success it became. The three of us absolutely coincided in our understanding of what doing the right thing meant. As a result, we believed that if we always followed the objectives of doing great work and looking after the people who worked for us, then there was a real opportunity to create a business that would endure and prosper. So there's the first lesson: always start a business with like-minded people you respect (and who aren't related to you!).

From Day One we made sure that fun was an important element in our particular mix. We laughed a lot. We played tennis, football, darts and snooker together. We worked hard but enjoyed ourselves as well – this was in the 70s long before dot.com start-ups thought they had invented such a workplace.

We agonised over the people who joined us, using the Bill Bernbach mantra of needing them to be nice as well as talented. We put more effort and time into recruitment than almost anything else we did, and we still do. We tried hard to prevent bullying. We showered praise where it was deserved and the occasional admonishments when they were required. We reasoned that if we created a great place to work, great people would want to come and work with us. Fortunately this turned out to be the case. The very best people in each of the advertising disciplines beat a path to our door, and during the first decade of the agency's life, only a tiny number of people left – and hardly any clients.

The unwritten Mission Statement at the heart of the agency from Day One was 'When in Doubt Be Nice'. This view of the world is at the core of what I believe about advertising, business and life in general. When I say 'nice' I mean, being reasonable, being understanding, listening, making time, valuing people, trusting people. Nice is not patting people on the head. It's every single person respecting every single other person. Do that and you create a great business for both the people who work in it and for the investors and shareholders. Take care of each other and everything else will take care of itself. It's a credo for life.

When creating a company culture, starting a business from scratch – as David, Adrian and I did – is an enormous advantage. You can hand-pick your early disciples who become fundamental in the creation of the next wave of employees who then become instrumental in influencing the next wave and so on. This is not as difficult as it sounds because fundamentally people want to emotionally belong to something whether it be family, friends, clubs or causes.

My own passion for football is a case in point. It is an important part in mine and many other people's lives. During the working week most fans have jobs working for companies they find it difficult to relate to because their opinions are neither sought nor listened to. But when Saturday comes their opinions about their team are as valid as anybody else's and they can express themselves without fear – and certainly do so. Fans believe in their team, they share a dream with other fans and even when that dream is temporarily shattered by failure they still remain devoted.

This hunger for things to believe in is something that we can carry into our business lives. If we create a set of principles and beliefs that the people who work for us can subscribe to then the benefit to be reaped is enormous. The opportunity is there to encourage and create a secure and highly productive workforce. I recognise that things are tougher today than in the heady days of the 1970s, but I'm convinced that the more difficult the circumstances, the bigger the benefit of creating a working environment which is both principled and driven.

The following pages illustrate how I refined my beliefs. They will, I hope, help you create a business culture which is comfortable, sustaining, more than a little exciting, and ultimately hugely successful. It is a collection of ideas which have come of age.

1
STARTING OUT

1 Oportunity and Strategy

Life is a mixture of opportunity and strategy, with opportunity being much more significant in the long run than strategy. The problem is opportunity can't be legislated for – by definition it catches you by surprise – so you have to have a vague strategic plan to go forward with, in the knowledge that opportunity will almost certainly interfere with it but not knowing exactly when.

I learned this lesson for the first time at the end of my school days when it was apparent that university was out of the question for me. My school had quite justifiably given up on me at the age of 16 and decided that I should talk to what was then called a Youth Employment Officer. This man, who sadly I never had contact with again, transformed my life. During our interview he asked what I would really like to do and I replied that I had no idea. Thoughts of being an airline pilot and other fanciful things were scuppered by my poor eyesight. However, an idea came to me. A few weeks earlier my father had bought our first record player, so my immediate response was to tell this man in my broad cockney accent that I'd like to join the promotions department of a record company so I could meet the stars.

He looked at me rather quizzically and said, 'You mean advertising.' I knew nothing about careers in advertising but the Youth Employment Officer did and that mattered much more. He gave me three introductory cards to advertising agencies and I wrote to them immediately. Not long after that, two of the agencies offered me a job in their despatch departments. That one conversation ultimately led me to create, with David Abbott and Adrian Vickers, what *Campaign* Magazine once described as, 'the most successful UK advertising agency of all time'.

NEVER BE AFRAID TO DEVIATE FROM A PLOTTED COURSE, NO MATTER HOW MUCH TIME, THOUGHT AND FAITH YOU'VE INVESTED IN IT, IF A LEFT-FIELD OPPORTUNITY COMES ALONG

2 Reverence and the Working Class

As a boy from South London, I grew up with a working-class overdeveloped sense of reverence for the 'boss classes'. It was only later that I realised you can revere the boss classes too much. They have to prove their judgement and ability the same as the rest of us.

Some of those things that I questioned early on but dismissed my doubts about, believing that greater minds than mine really were behind them, ended up going spectacularly wrong – the mergers of Time Warner with AOL and RBS with ABN-AMRO are just two examples of moments where greater minds than mine were definitely not at work! They demonstrated that being in a position of power does not always equal great judgement.

**BEING IN POWER DOES NOT
ALWAYS EQUAL GREAT JUDGEMENT**

3 What Alec Guinness Said to Mark Hamill

Do you remember in *Star Wars* when Obi-Wan Kenobi said to Luke Skywalker, 'Luke, listen to the force'? In business terms I've always believed that to mean 'Trust your instincts.' This is brilliant advice if you have great instincts but terrible advice if you have bad ones.

Try to find out early in your career (and life) whether your instincts can be trusted. If you're one of the fortunate few who do have good instincts, 'listen to the force'.

GREAT INSTINCTS ARE THE CRUCIAL DIFFERENCE THAT MOST SUCCESSFUL BUSINESSMEN POSSESS – SPEND AS MUCH TIME AS POSSIBLE HONING YOUR INSTINCTS

4 An Understanding Authority Figure Makes a Difference

The most dubious distinction I hold is having been chairman of a football club that was top of its division in December and relegated in May. To my knowledge, this is the only time it's happened in footballing history. My other distinction is that I was the first person to be declared redundant by the established advertising agency who were my first employers, S. H. Benson. For a working class boy this was an enormous shock, as well as being disappointing and a little frightening because I wondered if I would ever get such an opportunity again.

I received the news as stoically as I could manage and went home trembling to tell my dad. I arrived at our flat in south east London and rang the bell. He opened the door and said, 'What's happened? You look as if you've seen a ghost. You're as pale as a sheet.' I told him I'd just been given the sack. I was expecting anger but he said, 'Never mind, son, it's their loss. Come in and I'll make you a cup of tea.'

That moment helped me realise how a level of understanding from someone you respect and admire can make all the difference when you are in a vulnerable state. My father's words helped me feel better very quickly and I got a new job within two weeks. With my redundancy pay from eight years at my first agency and my new salary, I can't remember ever feeling as rich or as satisfied. Thanks Dad.

**UNDERSTANDING, ADVICE AND
SYMPATHY FROM SOMEONE YOU RESPECT
CAN MAKE AN ENORMOUS DIFFERENCE**

5 Find a Single Source of Advice and Stick with It

Recently a number of small companies have asked my advice about how to grow their business and what direction they should take. There is hardly anything more rewarding for someone who has founded and led a number of successful organisations than being asked for advice by fledgling companies.

The trouble is when they solicit not only my opinion but also ask three or four other ageing entrepreneurs for advice as well. It's absolutely sensible to get more than one outside view of your business and its prospects. However, the likelihood of four or five mentors agreeing on the way forward is so remote that only confusion will result.

FIND A TRUSTWORTHY SINGLE SOURCE OF ADVICE AND STICK WITH IT

6 Slicing the Cake

Every newly formed company has a nucleus of founders. These are the people who shoulder the pressure and in many cases the financial risks of trying to fulfil the dream of being their own boss and of building something which they hope will endure and prosper. The very best entrepreneurs will recognise they can't do it alone and should ensure the organisation's success by spreading the potential rewards within it. This is not only fair but commercially sensible because people who have a piece of the action are much more likely to engage and give of their all rather than feeling that they are constantly pushing themselves to make a tiny number of people rich.

Over the years I have had many conversations with people who were interested in selling their companies. Those who came to me and explained that they owned 90 per cent of the equity failed to capture my interest. It meant that they had not used the weapons of inclusiveness and equity to attract the very best people to drive their business forward.

EQUITY IN YOUR COMPANY WILL BE MUCH SOUGHT AFTER – USE IT TO CREATE A SENSE OF LOYALTY AND A DESIRE TO SUCCEED BUT DON'T GIVE TOO MUCH AWAY TO THE WRONG PEOPLE

TAKE A RISK BUT BE SURE YOU PICK THE RIGHT PEOPLE

By 1971, a whole series of events had conspired to bring me to the point of starting out on my own. There was no precedent of any Mead family members starting a successful business from scratch. Even my father had inherited the West End & District Window Cleaning Company from the man he had worked with for some 10 years. My dad had been dead for five years when I embarked on what was considered among my immediate family to be a somewhat foolhardy venture. I was reminded of a book one of the great creative people of the Mad Men era had written, which was called George, Be Careful. The man in question was George Lois, a member of the elite group who made up Doyle Dane Bernbach in the 60s. When he told his mother he was leaving she berated him, saying that nice Mr Bernbach had paid him a lot of money and what was to be gained by doing it himself? After he carefully explained his burning desire to try and change his particular world she did indeed say, 'George, be careful'.

My mother felt pretty much the same. She had seen me fly around Europe, drive an exotic motorcar and always appear to have money in my pocket. Like George with his mother, I tried to explain to her that there was a real opportunity to start up my own business. There was nowhere else I wanted to work – Collett's, the hottest agency in town, had already turned me down some years earlier.

You didn't need much money to start an advertising agency in those days and as I began to plan and work things out, I was reminded of one of my favourite old ads: Ernest

Shackleton's appeal in *The Daily Telegraph* for recruits to yet another Antarctic expedition. The copy, to paraphrase it, asked for volunteers for a hazardous journey in which the likelihood of failure was high but success would bring fame, recognition and rewards.

At roughly this time I met an inventor called Eddie Leshik. He told me how he had spent years developing a portable music system. It was based around a mini cassette, not unlike those used in dictating machines, and a battery driven player. His concept was a good 10 years in advance of Sony developing the Walkman and was very seductive. Although he never actually produced a working model, he maintained it was only a matter of time before his device would make all of us very rich. He needed marketing advice and believed that advertising for his wonder machine was absolutely essential. So the first client was sitting there waiting for the Mead project to see the light of day.

I had been encouraged by a couple of wealthy potential backers to start up for a while. I'd calculated that I needed just enough capital to finance the business for six months without any income from clients. This would obviously mean myself and my partners working for nothing during the initial start-up phase. Being single with no commitments other than to look after my mother's modest needs meant that this was a no-brainer for me. I thought the ideal set-up for our new company would be a copywriter and art director, a media man and another account man to help me trawl for new business.

The two agencies that had been very formative in my life to that point were KMP and DDB. The second account man and the media man, Neville Cruttenden and Mike Osborne respectively, came from KMP and, despite both being family men, counted themselves in instantly when I broached the subject with them. The creative team had to come from DDB and I knew exactly who I wanted. David Abbott by then had been made managing director or even chairman at the hothouse in Baker Street. He had spent the last few years working with Brian Byfield as his art director and they had produced a really impressive body of work, particularly on Volkswagen. But no matter how hard I tried I couldn't persuade David to come with me. He was doing extraordinarily well at DDB and had four kids under the age of 10 to provide for. Although passing on this particular opportunity, he was very useful in helping me to persuade Brian Byfield to join me. After lengthy meetings in my flat in Grove End Gardens and the recruitment of Paul Whelan, one of the really good, if somewhat intense, writers at DDB, our new venture was born.

The absence of David was a major blow but I figured that Brian had a stellar enough reputation to create a stir in the marketplace. We decided that democracy would be the guiding management philosophy for our fledgling company. This was epitomised by the name we chose. The agency was to be called Byfield, Cruttenden and Mead. I remember the meeting when this was decided. We had some letterhead dummied up and found ourselves an office just above the Post Office in Baker Street. With the money put in by my friends as backers, we secured the lease, and everybody gave in their notice at their respective companies. Although I had raised all of the money and was, I guess, the driving force behind the new company, I gave away 67 per cent of the equity to my four partners. Before we started, Byfield, Whelan and Osborne decided to oppose the name of the company and poor old Neville was removed from the letter-head. So Byfield Mead it was.

We had a great time in those early days, with the combined fear of failure driving us all on and within a week had a lead for our second piece of business – Mr Leshik and his miracle box being our founding account. Brian's aunt worked for a company called Medway Builders. Based in Rochester in Kent they were healthy competitors to the dominant company in portable office space at the time – Portakabin. She told us that she had been serving tea at a board meeting when she overheard that they were looking for a new advertising agency. Excited by this, we rushed off a letter to the managing director of the company and to our astonishment got a reply asking us to go down to the busy Kent town and present our credentials. We were halfway through this exercise in front of the whole board of Medway when the door opened and the tea lady came in. It wasn't Brian's aunt but her best friend at the company. When she'd dispensed cups to everybody, she turned to the chairman of the company and asked if he minded if she spoke to Brian. Mortified, the two of us stood there while she said, 'Brian, your Auntie May said when you finished maybe you'd pop into her flat on the way home for some tea and cake.' She then pushed her trolley out, leaving us believing that our chances of winning this piece of business had disappeared.

Astonishingly, this wasn't the case and we were appointed virtually immediately. Paul did some great ads, I wrote a headline, Brian got a great artist called Alan Aldridge to do some spectacular illustrations and we had our first double page spreads in colour in *The Sunday Times Magazine*. We were off and running. Our very first ads won creative awards at the following year's design and art direction competition.

I had written to the heads of all the major agencies in London announcing our existence and slightly begging for any crumbs that came their way – accounts that were too small for them could make all the difference to us. The *Financial Times* did a small piece at the time of our launch under the headline, 'Byfield Mead Minus Frills.' I'm still not sure what they meant but the publicity gave us all a warm glow.

Sadly we were brought up very short by Eddie Leshik getting into financial difficulties. We had spent about 10 per cent of our precious capital developing a campaign for him and his product for which we were never going to get paid. The buccaneering spirit of my partners, particularly Paul, evaporated almost overnight. I tried really hard to reassure everybody that things would be fine but it was a struggle and they were pretty dark days. A week or so later, I was sitting in my office after another uncomfortable session with the brooding copywriter when I got a call saying we had a chance to pitch to a company called United Rum Merchants (URM). The chairman was the father of an old friend of mine. We were briefed on a project called Santigo, which was yet another attempt to unseat Bacardi. The pitch was to look at the project from top to bottom. We designed the label and the shape of the bottle itself, together with a raft of advertising. We were competing against URM's other agency, FCB, who were situated just across the road from us in Baker Street. While they pitched in the morning we were on at three o'clock the same day.

When our meeting began, the sales and marketing director entered in a state of high dudgeon. He was outraged that on his arrival at FCB he had been given a cup of coffee in a paper cup. He found this both offensive and disrespectful. He told me this story while sipping from our Rosenthal china cups. At the end of our presentation, he told me that we were to be appointed and to this day I'm sure we won because of FCB's paper cups.

That was in the early autumn. Around Christmas time, at the lunch the client gave for both its agencies, the three FCB representatives made things even worse by ordering gin and tonics at the bar. Despite a very extensive repertoire of spirits, gin was the one product not in URM's portfolio. The three of us ordered Santigo and tonic. A sensible gesture, but it tasted disgusting.

Our first year in business flew by. We appointed a number of really good people but always ran the business conservatively to ensure that we could repay our initial backers and never had to use an overdraft. However, the flaws of running as a full democracy were beginning to emerge. Decision-making was tortuous and every small move forward had to be discussed and negotiated at length between the five of us. Also, all of us had worked on major pieces of business in our past agencies and felt that we were not being stretched either strategically or creatively on the accounts that we'd acquired. We needed a really significant advertiser to both enhance our reputation and give us a bigger canvas on which to paint.

Almost on cue came a telephone call which transformed our little agency. The sales director at British Leyland was a man called Michael Hellas, whom I had worked with on the Leyland business. He'd left the Longbridge giant and unbeknown to me had joined Thomas Tilling, a conglomerate who had the franchise to market Mercedes cars in the UK. He said they were looking for an agency and asked if I was interested. Barely able to contain my excitement, I said we'd be happy to go down and have a chat to see if there was any way we might work together.

All of us turned up for a two-hour meeting at the Mercedes headquarters on the Great West Road. It went very well and we could hardly believe that there was every possibility that the great German carmaker would be our first major client. Mike told me that they had another agency to see but that I shouldn't worry as they really liked what we had to say. But the following afternoon I got a call saying that it was bad news. The other agency had produced creative work which they quite liked so they were inclined to give them the business. Brian and I were devastated but it occurred to me that Michael had behaved in an uncharacteristic way.

So within half an hour of receiving his call, I rang him back and asked if he had told the other agency that they'd won. He said he hadn't but planned to do so imminently. I said I thought he'd behaved rather unfairly in that we hadn't had the opportunity to show what we could do for him creatively. He pondered for a moment and agreed that we could have 10 days to produce our own creative work. That meant if Thomas Tilling still chose the other agency, the whole exercise at least would have happened on a level playing field. We all worked every hour for the next week or so, particularly Brian and Paul, and produced a raft of really great ideas. After our presentation Mike took me aside and said we had the business. Although none of us were heavy drinkers we made an exception that night. We were off and running towards the big league – it was a wonderful feeling.

Since the beginning we had been banking with the Royal Bank of Scotland, and our initial capital injection meant our early expenditure was all covered. Even with Eddie's bad debt we had not had to call on them for any financial help, and with the acquisition of the Mercedes account we were making a slight monthly profit. To raise the capital to start the agency, all of us had got rid of our smart motorcars and were driving around in a motley selection of old bangers. As Thomas Tilling also owned the Audi franchise, we decided we would purchase Audis for the partners as those were the days when company cars were an integral part of anybody's package. This would entail a short-term loan of some £10,000. I went to see our bank manager in Burlington Gardens and put forward this proposition. It was immediately turned down.

Since the early days of the agency, a man called Jonathan Agnew had been chairman. He worked for a major merchant bank called Hill Samuel who had just started a retail operation based in very elegant offices on the corner of St James's Square. When he heard of our shabby treatment at the hands of RBS, he suggested that we go along to see a man called Ted Emerson who ran the first Hill Samuel retail branch. Within half an hour of meeting Ted, we had secured a loan for the Audis and had switched our business totally to his bank. Coupled with the appointment of Arthur Andersen as our auditors and Lewis Silkin as our lawyers, we had put together a very respectable lineup of advisers. In the decades that followed, Ted Emerson played a central role in my life for which I'll be eternally grateful.

7 The Umbrella of Affection

The best partnerships have what David, Adrian and I have described over the years as the 'Umbrella of Affection' binding them together. We were all incredibly fond of one another, which allowed each of us the freedom to criticise and bitch about the others, because we knew that the 'Umbrella of Affection' was inviolate. If ever push came to shove, what would decide the way forward would be the way we felt about one another. That affection bound the three of us and also worked as a force field. Nobody could pick us off one by one.

ANYTHING THAT BINDS PARTNERS TOGETHER IS INVALUABLE – AFFECTION IS ONE OF THE MOST POWERFUL GLUES

8 If You Hire Small Minds You Will Finish up with a Small Company

If you hire people with small minds and talent to match you will never create a great company. Managers often forget that they are only as good as the people they surround themselves with. If any manager is insecure, there is a risk they will hire people who they believe offer no threat to them and people who offer no threat will offer very little value either.

In a much-acclaimed book called *Apple*, written in 1997, the respected Wall Street journalist Jim Carlton outlines the failure of John Sculley to pick really good people after the board of Apple dismissed Steve Jobs. That whole mood crumbled under Sculley to a point where Carlton wrote at the conclusion of his book, 'In short the real question of Apple is whether it has any future at all.'

He went on to say, 'Can anyone stop it? Maybe Steve Jobs can. But the odds are good that he can do no more than slow the fall.' What Steve Jobs did on his return was to look around his people, pick the best ones and allow them their head (as much as Steve Jobs allowed anybody their head). Sir Jonathan Ive designed the curvy iMac which reversed the downward trend in Mac sales and the rest is history.

**SURROUND YOURSELF WITH
THE BEST PEOPLE AVAILABLE**

9 The Square Peg and the Round Hole

No matter how much trouble you take in hiring people you will make mistakes. There was a popular myth around that we at AMV, in the old days, never fired anybody – sadly this wasn't true. However careful you are in the interviewing process and when doing due diligence on candidates, every so often you will find yourself with someone in the organisation who doesn't work out.

Our view was always that the responsibility for things not gelling was at least as much our fault as the individual's because we would have spent a lot of time persuading that person that our company was the right place for them. In truth, the company was probably 60 per cent responsible for that person being employed. Once the square peg in a round hole situation had been realised it needed to be corrected promptly but as kindly as possible. We were always very generous with both time and money to allow the person in question to leave with their dignity intact. Recruiting the right people in the right structure was something I learned early on.

CORRECT YOUR RECRUITMENT MISTAKES EARLY AND ACCEPT YOUR SHARE OF THE BLAME FOR THINGS NOT WORKING OUT

10 Beware of Success – Egos Can Be Destructive

At the start of any new venture the participants are bound together by a common fear of failure. Importantly, this allows the subjugation of egos and avoids that familiar virus – resentment.

If you're not very careful, a modicum of success can destroy the togetherness that fear of failure engenders and turf wars can break out based on individual levels of recognition for that success. Surprisingly then, it is success that can split an organisation asunder if great care is not taken.

EARLY SUCCESS CAN BRING AS MANY PROBLEMS AS FEAR OF FAILURE – HANDLE EGOS VERY CAREFULLY AND REMEMBER THAT NAPOLEON ONCE SAID 'THE GREATEST DANGER OCCURS AT THE MOMENT OF VICTORY'

DON'T BE GREEDY

The early years of my first start-up, Byfield Mead, appeared to promise success. Despite coming from very different agencies, the combined cultures of the founders seemed to bind us together. We were early supporters of a new company called The Advertising Agency Register. Set up by a very energetic lady called Lyndy Payne, whom I'd known from my Benson days, it allowed clients to secretly look at agency offerings from the central register that the AAR had compiled. It proved very useful for us and a relatively steady stream of new business came in to see us. Our conversion rate was about 50 per cent, and within a couple of years, we found ourselves working for not only Mercedes and Medway Builders but for Canada Dry and Standard Brands (who had a new margarine product called Fresh Fields), together with a quasi-government appointment – the Milton Keynes Development Corporation.

Meanwhile, a good friend, Jennie Armstrong, whom I'd known for a number of years since we met as junior employees at Benson's, had become emotionally involved with a man called Peter Mayle. At that stage, along with David Abbott, he was viewed as one of the star copywriters in British advertising. Like David he was good-looking, urbane and very charismatic. He had started the UK operation of a hot US creative agency called PKL. This had been acquired by BBDO London, one of the offshoots of the New-York-based American operation. Peter was creative director of the enlarged entity but after a couple of years decided that turning the operation around would take too long and that a great idea would be to buy Byfield Mead to inject new energy and allow us to work together. Although the five founders of our small agency were getting on well enough, hairline cracks were beginning to show and the promise of being part of a much bigger operation appealed to us, largely because of the extra security we would have. BBDO were prepared to offer something just short of £250,000 for our agency, an enormous amount of money at that time for a business in its infancy. I flew to New York to meet with Bruce Crawford, the legendary head of BBDO Worldwide, and we seemed to get along fine.

But an element of greed set in and we collectively decided that we would push for another £50,000 and deputed Jonathan Agnew to negotiate directly with Bruce Crawford. This really was chalk talking to cheese. Bruce had always thought that the price he was offering was a premium but worth paying because the deal would help him sort out a problem in London and keep Peter Mayle happy. He didn't appreciate Jonathan's negotiating style and the deal died. On reflection, this moment was the beginning of the end of the agency. Even though a deal was not struck, during the negotiations people had already started emotionally spending the money they thought was coming their way. The hairline cracks in the relationships between the five of us started to become fissures and discontent started stalking the floors of our offices in Baker Street.

Around this time, relationships between the government and trade unions were at an all-time low, resulting in a number of strikes and leading to the slightly surreal situation of businesses only being allocated enough energy to operate three days a week. We continually had to decamp to the

Churchill Hotel in Portman Square to carry on trying to grow the business. At the same time, we were bursting out of our Baker Street offices and found a great site 500 yards away for our new premises. They backed on to a park diagonally across from what became AMV's offices years later. New business came in but the discontent, for which we were all responsible, grew. Brian and I pitched for an old piece of business that I had worked on previously – White Horse Whisky. It was truly one of the worst presentations that he and I had ever done together and on the way back in the taxi we berated one another for the awfulness of our performance. When I got back to my desk, there was a message waiting for me from the marketing director saying that they were blown away and the business was ours. It was a reminder of something that I learned many times over the years: that it is almost impossible to judge the result of a competitive pitch in advance of the decision being made.

We moved to our new office and for a while things settled down. We still had fractious board meetings. Every decision, no matter how small, had to be decided on a vote and factions emerged. The trouble was that at the following board meeting, factions emerged again but were differently aligned. Nonetheless, we carried on winning the odd piece of business, the agency's reputation grew and nobody had left us since the start. We'd also never had an overdraft.

The final nail in the coffin of Byfield Mead came with BBDO approaching us again with a view to merging. I had a call from the then CEO of the London office asking for a meeting. By then, Peter had left to go to New York with Jennie, where he was working on clients like Gillette in the agency's Sixth Avenue offices. The London CEO, a man called Mike McLoughlin, explained that he would like us to join him to once again try to revitalise their London operation. The British economy had worsened substantially since the offer of two years before and the new suggestion was to acquire us for 30 per cent less than the figure which had been at the heart of our earlier negotiations. We had just been put on a shortlist by our first million-pound account. I took the view that this meant we had broken through the awareness barrier and were developing a reputation amongst London's agencies that might result in relatively spectacular growth. This view was shared by one of my partners but the other three had had enough and instructed me to try to negotiate the best deal that I could. My heart wasn't in the negotiations and my opposition only served to exacerbate the widening gulf between the partners.

After a protracted and unpleasant period of negotiations with both BBDO and internally among the partners, the cracks became chasms. I became the lightning rod for the pent-up frustrations and anger of the partnership and it was decided I should leave. Writing this many years later, I fully accept my share of responsibility for the breakdown of the relationships between the five of us. The manner of our parting left an enormous amount to be desired, and the enforced acquisition of my 33 per cent shareholding for £11,250 was, I still believe, derisory and unfair. The agency that I had conceived and founded had a modicum of success over the next few years but never became a major force. It was eventually gobbled up by another London group and disappeared without trace.

11 Be Careful What You Wish for, the Price Can Be High

I was recently having a conversation with my youngest son about what he wanted to do in his future working life. We were discussing life balances and I said I believed ambition is the enemy of contentment, because the pursuit of high targets can lead to the creation of a driven nature that may never be satisfied. The price of a really successful career can be very high.

History is full of people who found this to be true. Two spring to mind. Howard Hughes was born rich but with an insatiable desire to prove himself to himself. He had an unbelievably stellar career in aviation and Hollywood as well as business in general, but could never satisfy the high level of achievement that he set himself. Despite his multimillions of both dollars and admirers, he died a lonely, paranoid old man in a darkened hotel suite in Las Vegas. The other man who appeared never to find true contentment was Jean Paul Getty; once the richest man in the world, he finished up lacking any sense of generosity either in spirit or material things. The Getty tragedy is that pretty much his whole family became infected and ultimately destroyed by his lack of largesse.

BE PREPARED FOR THE SACRIFICES THAT BUSINESS SUCCESS CAN DEMAND OF YOU

12 'In Order to Enjoy the Rainbow You Have to Put up with the Rain'

I know all of us in business would love a rainbow-filled existence because a rainbow means the sun is shining. Sadly life isn't like that. And nor is business, especially a business where you are one telephone call away from triumph or disaster. Putting up with the rain makes the rainbow even more enjoyable. A healthy understanding that the only good thing about getting wet is that you may be dry soon afterwards is well worth remembering. I'd love to claim the saying as mine, but Dolly Parton said it first.

BUSINESS LIFE IS A SUCCESSION OF UPS AND DOWNS – DON'T BE TOO ELATED OR DEFLATED BY THEM

13 You Never Get a Second Chance to Make a First Impression

Mae West, a very famous pre-war Hollywood movie star, is credited with this flash of insight. Throughout the history of my active involvement in the running of AMV, reception has always reported directly to me. I recognise the absolute importance of their role in our agency's life.

Over the years we have had some great reception figures. The first was a lady called Jan Elliott who spent 10 or 12 years with us. She was brilliant. When she left, one of the greatest characters AMV BBDO has ever produced took over from her. Pascoe was with us for well over 20 years and had an effortless elegance and style that could be fearsome if it wasn't allied to a wonderful humane manner and genuine concern for people's welfare. Since Pascoe we have had another 25-year veteran in Ingi Soliman, who is now on the board at the very heart of the agency.

The reception team are the first contact that prospective clients and employees have with our agency. I know it's incredibly difficult to quantify but I suspect more than one piece of new business owed rather more to the wonderful welcome than to the strategies and creative work which followed it.

FIRST IMPRESSIONS TEND TO BE INDELIBLE – MAKE SURE THEY'RE AS NEAR PERFECT AS POSSIBLE

2

STEPPING STONES

14 If You Don't Believe in it How Can I?

After my surprising and rapid rise through the ranks of my first ad agency, one day I had to go down to Hotpoint (a white goods manufacturer) whose offices were then very close to Buckingham Palace. The purpose of the meeting was to present for approval a relatively small advertisement that we had developed for one of their products for insertion in the Hong Kong newspaper the *South China Morning Post*. To my horror, the rather junior man who I should have presented to was away sick and I was ushered into the large office of the Worldwide Marketing Director. I was terrified as I passed over the advertisement for him to look at because I had done no preparation at all for selling it to him. He looked at it, peered over his glasses and said, 'What do you think?' I told him that I thought it was all right.

He then became quietly menacing and said to me, 'I never want you ever to come down here again with something that you think is "all right". If you don't think this is the best your company can produce and aren't prepared to say that in front of me, then I'm not prepared to give you the time of day.'

CONFIDENCE IN YOUR PRODUCT IS ESSENTIAL IN THE MARKETING PROCESS

15 Think Outside the Box

Sometime around 1988 I was introduced to a dynamic young PR person called Matthew Freud, and we bought his company too. The great-great-grandson of Sigmund, Matthew was extremely impressive and, much more importantly, wonderfully likeable. He remains to this day one of my closest friends even though we haven't been in business together for many years.

Early in our relationship we were given the task of informing the world that Pepsi were going to change the base colour on their cans to blue. We at AMV did the normal posters and a short television commercial. Matthew, on the other hand, with his PR hat on rented a Concorde from Air France, painted it blue, added the Pepsi logo on the side and created a huge number of photo opportunities. Astonishingly, he also persuaded the *Daily Mirror* to print on blue paper. It was the first occasion of many when he demonstrated how smart we were to buy him. To this day, however, I believe that on my first visit to his office he had non-staff seated at the desks to give me the impression the organisation was much bigger than it actually was.

THINK BIG, ESPECIALLY WHEN IT COMES TO CREATIVE WORK

16 The Objectivity of Ignorance

In the advertising business where we deal with many different clients, we invented the expression 'Objectivity of Ignorance'. Rather than immediately immerse ourselves in a potential client's business, we like to retain the 'Objectivity of Ignorance' for as long as possible. I suppose it might be akin to beginner's luck. That period when you don't overthink things and gut instinct is not subsumed in received wisdom and cluttered with information.

I'm not saying you should not know all there is to know about your clients and their customers. What I am saying is that at the beginning of a relationship we are as close as we ever get to being a consumer of that client's business. This is a magical time when your judgement is unimpaired by overfamiliarity or, much more importantly, political considerations. It's a time during which you can ask questions that you might later shy away from.

Algorithms are great at analysis but rubbish at creativity. In an age where Big Data, the role of Insight and social media analysis is king, it's easy to forget that the best piece of analytic equipment is the human brain and human instincts are at their freshest and most unsullied early in a business relationship.

**THINK LIKE A CUSTOMER
FOR AS LONG AS YOU CAN**

17 Creativity and All That

Ed McCabe, one of the greatest copywriters America has ever produced, said, 'Creativity is one of the last remaining legal ways of gaining an unfair advantage over your competition.' This is true of all of our businesses: creativity in the way we present our products to our consumers, creativity in the way we manufacture and creativity in the way we treat our people.

McCabe himself was faced with a really difficult creative problem when the agency won a very large piece of business from Perdue chickens. Chicken breeders had allowed themselves to be played off against one another and as a result the whole business had been defined by commodity/price considerations. Frank Perdue had an edge in that he fed his chickens a high-quality cereal that gave them a distinctly darker-skinned colour and a richer taste. But various agencies had tried to put this message across in believable terms and failed.

McCabe did two things: he created a tagline 'it takes a tough man to make a tender chicken' and at the same time noticed that Frank Perdue himself looked a bit like a chicken. Frank allowed himself to be parodied and as a result created a brand that consumers loved.

USE CREATIVITY TO AVOID BECOMING JUST ANOTHER COMMODITY

SAINSBURY'S

Soon after AMV moved to Babmaes Street, our first real offices, we got a call from Peter Davis who was the marketing director of Sainsbury's. In the first instance he came in to see David. He explained that, although they had successfully countered a major Tesco price initiative, he intuitively felt that they were falling behind in quality perceptions against Marks & Spencer. He said it was clear that they had to compete at both levels to maintain and build on their dominant position as a grocery retailer. He said he wanted to run a quality press campaign, mainly in the Sunday supplements, with all the emphasis being put on quality and innovation.

David and his long-serving art director Ron Brown took to this brief like ducks to water. David created an early agreement with Peter pledging to get Sainsbury's into every headline.

The *quid pro quo* for this was that we wouldn't have to have a giant logo at the bottom of each ad which would interfere with the quality feel of the layout. Fortunately, Peter readily agreed, and David and Ron embarked on the longest press campaign in grocery advertising history. In order to save money, Ken New, our brilliant media director, bought media in a very disciplined way. He firmly mandated that Sainsbury's would be the first food ad in any issue of any magazine that we appeared in. David and Ken also agreed that we would have a single page in colour facing a single page in black-and-white. We retained all the impact of a colour double page spread but the cost was significantly less.

In the early days Ron commissioned beautifully lifelike artist's renditions of the food subject matter. He decided quite quickly, however, that this added an unnecessary complication and cost in the production of the ads and discovered a magical food photographer called Martin Thompson who thereafter shot every Sainsbury's colour ad. Probably the most famous ad in the series was a shot showing a pack of minced beef with the headline, 'If Sainsbury's don't sell their mince in a day, they don't sell it.' It garnered a host of awards and set the style for hundreds of subsequent mini-masterpieces.

At some stage we were asked to translate our efforts in the press to television. This proved quite difficult until one day David said to the account team that he wanted to do recipes. I remember one of them coming to me expressing disappointment that this didn't seem like an earth shattering idea. I slightly agreed but said that we should let David demonstrate what he meant. David was a genius, after all. And I was not disappointed because in my view the campaign he and Ron produced literally changed the face of food advertising on television. They enlisted a director called John Clark, a very successful stills photographer who had turned his hand to directing commercials, and a series of beautifully shot TV ads resulted from this collaboration. The work they did was painstaking, the product of three perfectionists: John might take a day shooting the slicing of a tomato until it was absolutely perfect. The end frame of each commercial had a celebrity endorsing the recipe that had been shot and sales of each of the ingredients skyrocketed. Most of the television commercials we see today are an unashamed copy of David, Ron and John's efforts all those years ago.

Sadly the relationship with Sainsbury's ended in 2014 after 37 years. I genuinely think we knew more about the Sainsbury's brand than anyone, even those in the company. It will always be a major part of the agency's history and we each have an enormous amount to thank the other for.

18 Revere Your Consumers

Over the last 25 years the ability for companies to distribute their products through a large number of different outlets has substantially reduced. The rise of supermarkets and retail chains, not to mention the internet, means the range of distribution channels available for most products has narrowed alarmingly, to the extent that in some cases no more than three major players dominate the distribution and sale of items in a product category. These players have become enormously powerful and quite often it is they who are deciding your marketing plan and not you. There is a way to fight this – and the way is to persuade consumers to demand your products.

Years ago I remember a man called Derek Reeve, who was then running Walkers Crisps – a relatively new company which had grown remarkably rapidly by producing a better product which was competitively priced. One day they got a call from one of the large supermarket chains (not the one we were involved with for decades) who told them that the way they supplied their product was no longer acceptable and the configuration had to be changed. The supermarket chain heard nothing back for four weeks and then rang Derek Reeve himself to say that they hadn't had a response. He said Walkers would need about eight months to adapt the way they shipped their product, to which the supermarket replied they wanted it done immediately. Derek said his company couldn't do that and the supermarket bluntly told him if that was the case then Walkers Crisps would be delisted.

To their surprise, Derek said that would actually work out well for his company because they had a lot of small independent shops who wanted to stock their product and, because of the high volume of sales through the supermarket, Walkers were unable to meet their demands. Delisting would enable Walkers to supply all those small independents. Within a week the supermarket rang back and said they were happy to wait for eight months and in the meantime, they would like Walkers to supply their product in the same old way. The moral of this story is the supermarket totally understood that, if they didn't stock Walkers Crisps, their customers would go elsewhere.

Increasingly in an age where consumers are shopping blind on the internet, the value of a brand is becoming the only weapon against commoditisation. At a time of dubious reviews, a product's brand identity and reputation are critical elements in the marketing process.

IF YOU ARE FORTUNATE ENOUGH TO HAVE A RECOGNISABLE AND TRUSTED BRAND, GUARD IT AT ALL COSTS

19 Value What You Do

A few years ago Tom Vyner, the then chief executive of Sainsbury's and one of our major clients, retired and I took him out for a farewell lunch to say goodbye. At the end of the lunch I thanked him for being such a great client. He gave me a puzzled look and asked me what exactly I meant. I said that he'd been tough but that always brought good work out of us and he'd supported us at times when the people who worked for him had tried to rein us in.

He said that I had misunderstood the relationship and asked me how much difference I thought the work we had done for him and the company over the years had made to his business. Before I could answer he said the benefits that his company had received from the relationship were incalculable but could be measured in tens of millions, if not hundreds of millions of pounds.

There are too many people in business generally who don't value what they do enough. How can you possibly get a good return for your efforts if you can't quantify the difference those efforts make?

RECOGNISE THE TRUE VALUE OF YOUR WORK

20 Smiths Crisps and the Value of Individual Relationships

Quite early in the agency's life we won the iconic UK brand, Smiths Crisps. It had fallen into some disrepair and, along with other snack brands Golden Wonder and KP, it found itself being used almost as a commodity brand by the distribution chain. It was owned by Nabisco Foods, a giant American food company. Soon after we acquired the business we were told that the head of Nabisco Canada was being jetted in to add new energy and drive. Although he had worked for Nabisco Canada for a number of years, Stan Heath was a Brit. Almost the first thing he did when he landed on these shores was to ring and ask for a full presentation from us on where we had got to with our market assessment and creative directions.

At the beginning of our presentation he was icily polite and listened attentively although I felt his mind was elsewhere, which was obviously worrying for us. At the end of our meeting in the late afternoon I asked him what his plans were for that evening. He said he had nothing on as he was alone in town and so I offered him dinner. We arrived at the restaurant at seven o'clock and left at midnight. Sometime during the evening he told me that he had come up to AMV to fire us. He had quite a lot of experience in dealing with the head of one of the major American agencies in town. He said that he trusted this person and that's the way he operated. He was in a hurry, he said, and he needed an advertising partner who would share his sense of urgency but particularly be someone he could work with. We left the restaurant with him offering a new extended contract to us as long as I would look after him. He was a great bloke so it was not difficult to agree to join him in his adventure.

Stan and I became great personal friends and together we drove his business forward. We were ruthless about the new product program that was underway at the Reading complex, reviewing existing products that could benefit from support as well as new introductions. Stan was a great client and an eager participant in the advertising process.

A particular incident stands out. One day I drove to Reading to present a rough cut of the commercial we'd produced for a product called Potato Tubes. Sadly it was an unmitigated disaster. An idea that looked great in script form just didn't translate into film. Stan asked my opinion and I said we couldn't run the commercial. He raised the question of its cost and I said it was his call. He responded by saying he would pay for the commercial if we sacrificed our mark-up. With indecent haste I agreed and asked him why he had been so generous. He said that two things were important. Firstly, we were partners and we had both agreed that it was worth the risk to try and make the idea work on film, which meant its failure was down to both of us. Secondly, and much more significantly, he said that creativity was enormously important to him in his product category. If he were to penalise us for being adventurous now then the next time a brilliant but off-the-wall idea was suggested at the agency it might get stifled at birth because of the financial risk. He absolutely did not want that to happen.

The upshot of all this was that every creative man in the agency wanted to work on Smiths. Some great commercials followed and we revitalised the brand. Stan was no pushover but he loved creativity, he always said thank you and absolutely insisted that his team treated our team with respect. Many years later, after his return to Canada, he had a fatal heart attack in his car on the way to the office. He is one of the people who will be remembered most fondly in Abbott Mead Vickers.

CREATIVITY IS FOSTERED BY PARTICIPANTS ON BOTH SIDES OF THE PROCESS – FREEDOM TO TAKE RISKS WILL PRODUCE MORE SUCCESSES THAN MISTAKES

21 Affection and Nostalgia Make Great Marketing Weapons

Within all manufacturing companies there are discarded and disregarded jewels. When we first began working for Smiths Crisps they had a very expensive new product development operation – I think there were at least 30 products being developed for market test. The last time I looked at any meaningful statistics, only about 5 per cent of any new products become winners. Smiths had long been famous for a product that could be described as 'salt and shake'. The unflavoured crisps came in a pack with a little blue bag of salt. There was a great deal of latent affection for this particular product because people remembered it fondly from their youth.

We reintroduced it and it was a roaring success. It required none of the excessive costs and manpower needed to sweat a new product on to the marketplace and I seem to remember it had the highest margins of any product in the portfolio at that time. Now that salt seems to be only just below arsenic on a list of substances that are bad for you, it might not work so well today but there are literally hundreds of products gathering dust that could be reintroduced and bring about the twin rewards of joy and profit.

**OLD PRODUCT DEVELOPMENT
IS JUST AS IMPORTANT AS NEW
PRODUCT DEVELOPMENT**

22 The Business of 'No'

More and more people are being given the power to say 'No' and conversely fewer and fewer have the ability to say 'Yes'.

I remember once sitting with the then chief executive of Millwall Football Club. We had built a brand new stadium, one end of which we had to devote to Away supporters. That end was capable of housing 4,500 people but quite often the clubs we were playing would only bring 200 supporters. So we were faced with an empty end at our stadium and relatively cheap seats behind the goal that our supporters could not use. I asked the chief executive to look at reconfiguring the stadium so that we could use that empty stand for our fans and re-house the Away supporters elsewhere. He gave me a response that I haven't forgotten to this day: 'Let me think why that's not possible'.

There are far too many people in management at lower levels these days who spend valuable time and energy trying to work out why something is not possible instead of trying to make things happen. The real problem is that a positive response made to any suggestion can seem to constitute responsibility for that decision – negativity in some people's minds equates to staying alive to fight another day.

**GET TO THE PEOPLE WHO CAN SAY 'YES'
AND AVOID THOSE WHO CAN ONLY SAY 'NO'**

23 *The Economist* and Involvement of Top Management

After we had moved to our offices in Aybrook Street, we pitched for this great British magazine. Under its relatively new CEO, David Gordon, it was making great strides and wanted to substantially increase the readership of each issue. We won the business. Abbott, Mead and Vickers sat down after Adrian received the call and the three of us decided that it was maybe too small an account for us at that stage in our development after all. Adrian was told to make the call to say, 'Thanks but no thanks.'

David Gordon himself intervened and persuaded us to take the business and he was so right. After a series of elegant long copy ads, David produced the first of an incredibly long-running series with white type on a red background echoing the magazine's masthead. 'I never read The Economist – Management trainee. Aged 42' was the message. It spawned award winner after award winner and meant that *The Economist* dominated the poster business for many years. The experience illustrates how the agency/client relationship is at its best when the very top management get involved in their campaigns. How they communicate with their customers is a critical part of their business.

There are many other great success stories of chief executives making profound decisions about the message they wanted to put out to the world. From Robert Townsend who approved the DDB campaign,

'Avis – we're number two so we try harder' through to Steve Jobs's 'Think Different', we see that, more often than not, great advertising and enlightened heads of organisations go hand-in-hand.

GETTING THE LEADERSHIP ON BOARD CAN MAKE ALL THE DIFFERENCE

24 Maybe They're Right

Much has been made of Bill Bernbach's influence on the advertising profession in the 60s and 70s. Alongside the great creative work he generated from his agency, he had a firm belief in the way his company should operate and conduct itself.

In those days people thought that there was an arrogance to DDB but in fact, Bill advised anybody presenting a piece of work to a client to have in a pocket an imaginary piece of paper bearing the words, 'Maybe they're right'.

Bill argued that a good idea doesn't mind who had it as long as it sees the light of day.

**ALL PARTICIPANTS SHOULD HAVE
AN INPUT IN THE CREATIVE PROCESS**

25 Learn How to Take 'Yes' for an Answer

I have presented many pieces of work to clients. On a number of occasions the first glimpse of the creative treatment has met with instant approval.

For some of my junior colleagues this wasn't particularly acceptable because they had spent a great deal of time marshalling arguments and justifications for the work and wanted to ensure these were not wasted. On the odd occasion, I have seen defeat snatched from the jaws of victory by advocates spending so much time explaining why a particular path had been adopted that the client started to question their first impression.

In my view, the second somebody says 'yes', that's the signal to pack the art bags, click the briefcases and beat a hasty retreat.

**RECOGNISE WHEN THE
VICTORY HAS BEEN WON**

YELLOW PAGES

Sainsbury's and Volvo were two of the cornerstones of the early years of Abbott Mead Vickers and they were joined soon after by Yellow Pages. Owned by British Telecom, the enormous directory business was all-powerful in the days before Google came along and changed the world. Millions of copies of their fat yellow books were delivered to households in the UK. For years they had a mnemonic in their television advertising which was the walking fingers image and the slogan 'Let your fingers do the walking'. We were approached to pitch for the business against four other big agencies. Yellow Pages was then a massive television advertiser and absolutely the sort of account we needed at that stage of AMV's development.

The main client contact was a man called John Condron. An impish Northern Irishman, he lived and breathed the paper powerhouse. We were comprehensively briefed and told to go away and map out the future. The product itself had been positioned as something that everybody could turn to in times of emergency. I seem to remember that the most used categories were plumbers, electricians, roofers and the like. The business model was very simple: for an extra fee more ambitious tradesmen could buy display advertising to help them stand out from the crowds who had normal listings on a single line of type. Any emergency orientated tradesmen would make sure that they were represented in up to a page of their own advertising.

The pitch team was led by David, myself and Leslie Butterfield, our planning director. We recognised that although Yellow Pages had enormous awareness, it had few friends among its consumers. It was seen as something to turn to only at a time of trouble and I remember at the time we compared it to a visit to the dentist. You would only go when the toothache became intolerable and you would leave saying, 'I hope not to see you again soon.' We reckoned that if we could turn Yellow Pages into a friend of the family, usage would rocket and our ability to extend the number of people taking display advertising would also go through the roof, if you'll pardon the expression.

Around that time CD players had just been introduced in the UK. As a lifelong gadget freak I was desperate to find one. Despite numerous trips up and down Tottenham Court Road, which was then the electrical gadget centre of London, I had no luck. One day sitting in my office playing with the Central London Yellow Pages directory, which was about three inches thick, I turned to the electrical retailer section and started making calls in the hope of tracking down the new breakthrough in music delivery. On my fourth call, I found a stockist in the Edgware Road who had one Hitachi player in stock and I asked him if he would keep it for me until I could get to him. Later that day I completed the purchase and I was beside myself with excitement. I relayed this story to David and he thought that the credit I gave Yellow Pages for making me happy was a pretty potent route to follow.

David wrote two commercials. One featured an old man called J. R. Hartley looking for a book he had written many years before on European butterflies, while the other had a doting dad trying to find a pony as a birthday present for his daughter. David commissioned a very emotional piece of music and enlisted the voice-over talents of Joss Ackland to pronounce the magic words, 'Good old Yellow Pages. We don't just help with the nasty things in life, like a blocked drain. We're there for the nice things too.'

David had to go away so on my birthday, after Leslie had produced a compelling strategic argument for our route forward, I read out the scripts and played the music and voice-over. That was pretty much it for our pitch. We had put all our eggs into one strategic basket which for us showed a lot of promise.

There were 12 people in the room from Yellow Pages. The boss of bosses was a man called Richard Hooper who had a very distinguished subsequent career, and Derek Dobie was John's immediate boss. We finished the presentation and encouraged questions. We were told none would be forthcoming and the decision would be made within the week.

On Friday afternoon at around six o'clock I got a call from Derek asking if he and John could come in and see me. It was rare in those days to receive a fee to do a new business pitch but characteristically Derek and John had said that £5,000 would be given to every losing agency to cover some of their costs. They arrived in my office with sombre faces and turned down my offer of tea. Derek started the meeting by reaching into his briefcase and producing a cheque made out to Abbott Mead Vickers for £5,000.

He made to pass it over but then, like Chris Tarrant on *Who Wants to Be a Millionaire?*, snatched it back before I could take it and said, 'You won't be needing that. We are giving you the business.' He then reached back into his briefcase and pulled out a bottle of champagne to celebrate. It was a wonderful way to end the week. Changing the J. R. Hartley commercial from European butterflies to fly fishing and the pony commercial to the purchase of a bike were the only alterations we had to make to the work we put forward at the new business presentation. Many, many years of Yellow Pages commercials were an absolutely carbon copy of the structure of those first two commercials.

I really believed that in our positioning of Yellow Pages as a friend of the family, we created a genuine bond not just with our users but with our advertisers as well. Every year when renewal time came around for retailers, I think they ticked the box for yet another 12 months of advertising because they felt they had a relationship with the directory. I will always believe that once that link was broken, coupled with the advent of electronic directories, the population's love affair with Yellow Pages ceased.

26 Be Gracious in Defeat...

Success or failure is only a telephone call away. By definition we are constantly presenting to win new business or defending our existing business.

Many years ago one of our great British institutions, British Airways, with a large prestigious advertising account, appointed a new chairman: Lord King. He was tasked with shaking up the business that at that point had become a bit moribund. He needed to make, or so he believed, a momentous decision early on to demonstrate his 'new broom' credentials. He fired his existing advertising agency and appointed a new one. Though patently unfair, this is a risk that agencies face daily.

The CEO of the fired agency held a press conference and attacked the wisdom and unfairness of the decision. The new agency that picked up the windfall from this major client had a disastrous first six months as custodian of the great brand. To this day I remain convinced that if the existing agency had remained sanguine about their dismissal in the face of such extreme provocation, the client would have come back cap in hand during that first six months.

Being gracious in victory isn't a bad tip either. When I was chairman of my beloved Millwall Football Club, I made sure that on the odd occasion when we won an

Away game we would, after the match, accept our host's hospitality and then leave as soon as was decent. This would allow no triumphalism on our part to pervade their boardroom but more importantly allow them to grieve in private.

BE GRACIOUS BOTH IN DEFEAT AND IN VICTORY

3
MANAGEMENT

27 Finding Good People
– a Grind as Well as a Talent

The single most significant success factor in our agency has been the quality of the people we've recruited in our quest to be the best, and finding them can be both a talent and a grind.

My experience is that you know whether somebody might not be right almost as soon as you begin an interview – it usually takes about 30 seconds and feels instinctive. By extension, if the interview goes on longer than planned, then it's also likely that the person in front of you will be interesting as a potential addition to your happy band of brothers and sisters.

However, after using your instincts to work out who might be a contender, the grind begins. You should then expose the potential employee to as many people as possible whose judgement you respect. Eventually you will narrow the field down to your chosen candidate. As in every other area of leadership and management, someone has to make the final decision. But in recruitment I've always found it really useful to have input from people I trust before that decision is made.

**SUCCESSFUL RECRUITMENT
RELIES ON INSTINCT AND INPUT**

28 What Motivates the People Who Work for You?

The very best company chiefs have an ability to read the people who work for them and understand that there is no universal rule for discovering what motivates them. But demonstrating care for people as individuals is often powerful.

I recently read the history of *Saturday Night Live,* the enormously successful New York TV show. After it had been running for a year, the first host, who had become extremely popular, said he was going to leave to make movies. This was a hammer blow to all concerned. He did indeed leave but in an interview many years later admitted, 'And you know if the boss had put his arm around me and given me a hug and asked me to stay, then I probably would have. But he didn't.'

People are motivated by different things. Some need driving on while others need an arm round the shoulder. But almost everybody needs to feel wanted. On the other side of the process, it's often fear of rejection that stops most people from saying what they really mean. Maybe that was the case with the *Saturday Night Live* boss all those years ago.

**UNDERSTAND THAT PEOPLE RESPOND
TO DIFFERENT MOTIVATIONS**

29 Rambo and Uriah Heep

I was once in a large meeting with a major UK retailer. The whole board was present and we were receiving a presentation from a highly respected forecasting unit about the consumer we were likely to face in the 21st century. The presenter went into a great deal of detail about the demographics, tastes, characteristics and requirements of this critical constituency. At the end of his presentation I asked what we expected of the 10,000 people who worked for the organisation, mostly in its shops? What imaginary uniform did they put on when they came to work each day? How did we expect them to represent the company?

The personnel director turned to me with a rather pitying look on his face and said, 'You should understand that we deal in high turnover low cost personnel.' This didn't really answer my question. However, I concluded he meant that he took the view that the staff were expendable and replaceable so there was no point giving them any directions on how to behave with customers. I felt then and still do that this was a policy of despair.

I've often made it clear to the people who worked at AMV that I would not want them to be like Rambo in attitude but I didn't want them to be Uriah Heep either. A pride in working for the company should not translate into either arrogance or obsequiousness.

Quiet confidence and an understanding of what our company representsand how important our customers are is the way forward.

MAKE SURE EVERY MEMBER OF YOUR STAFF REFLECTS THE COMPANY ETHOS

30 An Unfair Share of Heads and Hearts

When Abbott Mead Vickers became a public company, my role was to go and talk to analysts and fund managers in the City to explain the reasons why they should invest in our company. I wanted them to be secure in the knowledge that their investments were in good hands. I told them that I thought running a people business like ours was about capturing an unfair share of people's heads and hearts so that they give of their best.

In simple terms, if the people in your company are spending 50 per cent of their time feeling worried about their future, politicking or being psychologically bullied, then the other 50 per cent of their time is all the productivity you can expect from them and even that will be tainted. If you can create a workforce where 75 per cent of your employees' head is devoted to your company and, at the same time, twin that share of their head with a real affection for the company (and what it stands for), then the levels of productivity you get in return are mind-blowing. It's really very straightforward.

AN EMOTIONAL AS WELL AS RATIONAL RELATIONSHIP WITH YOUR COMPANY IS THE PERFECT COMBINATION FOR EMPLOYEES

31 Staff Retention and How to Do it

A company that I am involved with were very worried about their inability to retain their staff and had looked at all sorts of methods and advice about staff retention. Once we sat down and talked about the problem, it didn't take long to discover that the issue was not staff retention, it was staff recruitment.

What they had been doing was not taking enough time and trouble over employing people in the first place. They had been allowing people to come into their company without clearly understanding what the company's objectives were, its method of operation, or even the job specification itself. They were confusing activity with progress (page 92). Not surprisingly they were losing a lot of people who felt they had been sold the wrong bill of goods when they started work at the company.

They are now taking much more trouble over recruitment and I know that retention will immediately be better and, importantly, recruitment costs will go down. For every senior employee who stayed an extra year, we calculated they would probably save in excess of £50,000.

STAFF RETENTION STARTS AT THE BEGINNING, NOT THE END

32 The Accession to the Throne

There comes a time for lots of people when they are promoted to a level where they acquire responsibility for the welfare and advancement of others. All too often those who have been given the stripes of power assume that people's attitudes towards them – and the way they behave towards those people – should change without any more than a piece of communication having been sent to their new constituency.

Of course people's attitudes will have changed – but not in the way the person in power thinks or perhaps wants. Those people will be looking for indicators that the promotion was deserved and hoping they have got somebody as their superior who they feel able to follow. This is a time when the newly anointed have to recognise one absolute truth: respect has to be earned, before it can be commanded.

**RESPECT HAS TO BE EARNED
BEFORE IT CAN BE COMMANDED**

33 The Title Race

For many years British business resisted the temptation to follow the American route and have a myriad of job titles spread through the upper echelon of businesses. 'Chairman' and 'managing director' were the only two titles of any note. However, over the last decade or so UK management has given in. Business cards now carry a bewildering array of titles which by and large are bestowed either to smooth an ego or to negate the need for a salary increase.

When I ran AMV I resisted the temptation to have associate directors, in those days a very fashionable titbit to offer people. I reasoned that if I made a whole bunch of people associate directors, on their appointment they would immediately start a campaign to be made full directors. Meanwhile, the rest of the organisation would aspire to an overnight promotion to associate director. Rather than solving any problems, in this case expediency would have created a whole lot more. This is another example of the ripple effect, something which managers of people absolutely must understand if they are to be successful.

MEANINGLESS JOB TITLE IS NEVER THE SOLUTION TO AN ONGOING PROBLEM

34 Bonuses and How They Can Be Divisive

It is strange how bonuses can often create politics and dissention instead of being a happy reward for everyone who got one.

AMV used to have a rule which said that everybody in the organisation was given the same percentage of their salary as a bonus. After all, if everyone didn't contribute towards the organisation's success then they shouldn't be a part of it and, if they did contribute, they had every right to share in the rewards.

Inevitably this system meant the most valued employees took home more money because they earned more money in the first place, but the strict rule meant there was a sense of fairness about the process: everybody was happy rather than feeling hard done by or wanting to argue about why their bonus should be more than anybody else's. Today this system has fallen into disrepair almost everywhere and bonuses are targeted much more narrowly.

There seems to be a conceit in big companies that the board and CEOs are some sort of breed apart who are much more responsible for the success – though often not the failure – of a company. They have remuneration committees who seem to be part of the problem. The spurious argument that we have to pay highly in a global market is trotted out by the Institute of Directors and company MDs in the media all the time. Bonuses have become a right rather than something that is earned.

When the top of a company acts in this way it both sends the wrong signal that this is the right thing to do and encourages employees to emulate the top brass. A spiral of greed can ensue. Principled people lose heart and leave.

MAKE SURE BONUSES REFLECT EFFORT NOT ENTITLEMENT

35 The Importance of a Clean White Suit

The Rodgers and Hammerstein musical *South Pacific* tells the story of a group of American servicemen defending a Pacific island in World War Two. There are only a tiny number of women on the island, a situation which becomes a constant source of complaint from the troops. One memorable line in 'There's Nothing Like A Dame' says, 'There's nothing to put on a clean white suit for.' In the song this only refers to the lack of ladies to impress, but I believe it is also a life lesson.

If business life gives you nothing to put on a clean white suit for, then you are doomed. Most early retirees give up putting on any suit at all and their days become mildly pointless. As Henry David Thoreau once said, 'None are so old as those who have outlived enthusiasm.' Life and commerce are driven by the desire to put on the white suit; in other words to have purpose.

**EACH DAY SPENT IN BUSINESS
SHOULD HAVE A PURPOSE**

36 Blackadder and Baldrick – Master and Servant or Co-dependent?

The social order portrayed by Rowan Atkinson CBE and Sir Tony Robinson in their respective roles in *Blackadder* should not be a blueprint for any employer/employee relationship. The brutality, derision and contempt heaped on the unfortunate Baldrick is not what enlightened 21st-century industrial relations should look like. However, beneath the obvious comedy of the situation, a critical truth exists: Blackadder could not survive without Baldrick.

When applied to any organisation it should be understood that this mutual dependency is critical. Businesses cannot survive without people whose ambition is limited to being the best at what they do, no matter at what level they operate. Any company needs great foot soldiers who have no desire to be generals but just want to get the job done. These people should be cherished and looked after just as much as the high-flyers because without them nothing is possible.

**CHERISH YOUR FOOT SOLDIERS
AS MUCH AS YOUR HIGH-FLYERS**

37 Understand How Important it is to Listen

Many years ago when AMV was partnering SMS in New York, we helped on a campaign they were producing for a giant computer company called Sperry. Regrettably, like most of the big mainframe computer manufacturers, Sperry no longer exists. At that time, however, it was pitting itself against the might of IBM – 'The Big Blue'.

The dominance in the marketplace that IBM had created had made it somewhat unpopular with its customers. There was a feeling that it had become too big for its big blue boots and a sense that IBM felt it was doing people a favour by allowing them to buy its product. That meant there was a niche for a rather more sympathetic approach to potential buyers. We decided to position Sperry as the computer company that listened to its customers' requirements rather than shoehorning those requirements into available products. We embarked on a companywide program aimed at teaching people at Sperry how to recognise what a customer was saying. The campaign theme was, 'We understand how important it is to listen.' It was successful and for a time actually halted the Sperry decline.

That concept of 'understand how important it is to listen' remains as true today as it ever was, and is relevant to almost every aspect of business life. My experience from sitting in probably thousands of meetings over the years is that at least half the participants weren't listening to what other people said and were spending their time thinking of what they themselves were going to say next. The irony is that at least half the people present wouldn't listen to them either. When reviewing the contents of meetings I've often been astonished to discover how few people had been listening intently. Many problems that occur could have been nipped in the bud by lending an ear to what was going on.

Incidentally, you will know you have become a good listener when somebody says they have just shared something with you which they have never told anyone before. It's happened to me a few times and it's a wonderful compliment.

MAKE SURE EVERYONE
LEARNS HOW TO LISTEN

38 Little Things Mean a Lot

Over the years AMV has learned that the principle of 'it's the thought that counts' is as important and useful in business as it is in one's personal life. Every company should devote a small budget and a couple of genuinely concerned people to the simple job of making people feel better. As we move inexorably towards a less cohesive workforce, anything that can bring everybody together will be more valuable than ever before.

When we started our agency, we made enormous attempts to demonstrate how much we valued the people who worked for us. At Christmas, as well as a bonus, we would buy everybody an individual present selected by either David or myself. We made sure that people got handwritten notes of thanks for any special effort they made on our behalf. Once a year everybody and their families were taken out to a country club for a day where everybody mingled. As the agency got bigger and bigger it became more difficult to sustain some of these items but they were replaced by special events within the agency itself and above all the handwritten notes of thanks remained.

I encountered one problem area after David and Adrian retired. Previously, when people had worked at the agency for 10 years, they were given a stainless steel Cartier watch as a thank you. This was changed a few years ago to people being given money in order to buy their own watch – the thought was that this gave them ultimate flexibility. Although the sum matched what was spent on the Cartier watches, it missed the point of showing a long-term member of staff how valued they were. Most people given money would use it to pay the sort of pressing bills that all of us face instead. Replacing the watch with money reduced the impact of the gesture. Even if a staff member disliked the watch, they would always remember that they were given one.

ALWAYS REMEMBER IT'S
THE THOUGHT THAT COUNTS

39 People are More Important than Machines

In 1960, in the early days of my career, the second floor of Benson's eight-storey building was ripped apart and a huge room was created. After months of toil and expense, the magic day arrived when into the room was delivered the agency's first mainframe computer. I suspect it had no more capacity than a smartphone has today. This gleaming monster was housed in a dust-free air-conditioned environment – the only place in the building that afforded such comfort. I remember being astonished when passing by to see the cool, gleaming, humming monster sitting comfortably while the two people who operated it sat perspiring in their little offices just outside. I thought if we can't treat our people as well as we treat our machines then we deserve to reap the whirlwind.

Although this was many years ago, our love affair with technology has continued at a pace unthinkable even as recently as the 1990s. The digital age has transformed the way we work as well as the way we live. There is a real danger that we will become programmers to enable machines to carry out the creative functions that until now have been humankind's domain. With Artificial Intelligence becoming more of a reality with every day that passes, we must create an environment that is beyond electronic serfdom.

PEOPLE MATTER MORE THAN MACHINES

40 Pass Praise On

It has always been my practice to pass on nice things that a third party has said to me about somebody we both know. It's a terrible waste telling me how great somebody is if the person under discussion never learns of their standing.

Obviously if the praise is given and I'm told not to reveal it, I won't. But for the most part it's just forgetfulness on the part of the praiser to the praised. Something that could make an enormous difference to a person's life doesn't get communicated – how sad is that?

MOST PEOPLE NEED TO HEAR APPROVAL/RECOGNITION OF THEIR EFFORTS, FROM WHATEVER SOURCE

41 Sticks and Stones and All That

The saying 'sticks and stones may break my bones but names will never hurt me' is the most absurd expression in the English language. In reality, if I hit somebody and create a bruise, then that bruise will disappear, probably within 48 hours. If, on the other hand, I use names or words or even silence to attack the same individual, the psychological damage might last forever.

It's the same in business. Intimidation is not a good way to get the best out of people, nor is it the best way of building a business. In the 1960s the American firm Doyle Dane Bernbach was the most famous advertising agency in the world. Until DDB appeared on the scene, American advertising was known for its blunt, even bullying tone. The classic USP (unique selling proposition) approach favoured by Rosser Reeves at Ted Bates had been carrying all before it for decades. The theory was that you would find something unique and original to say about a product and then say it relentlessly, almost beating people over the head with that message in the hope that it would lead them to buy the product.

But DDB changed all that. It used charm and humour to get over powerful selling messages and quickly became the talk of Madison Avenue. As I began to look at my next career step, I was aware that I had a lot to learn about this alternative and creative approach to advertising. Somebody gave me an introduction and

I went for an interview at their offices at 62–64 Baker Street, later the site of a fashionable French restaurant called Galvin's. Amazingly, after what I thought was a poor interview with a rather stuffy head of client services, I was offered a job as an account manager on two of the most famous DDB worldwide clients. They were Volkswagen and Chivas Regal, both multi-award winners for the unique advertising created for them by the New York office. The new job gave me a chance to get involved in real creative advertising and led me to a life-changing meeting with David Abbott, who was to play such a central role in my life, as well as the rest of my advertising career.

DO NOT ALLOW ANY FORM OF BULLYING, PSYCHOLOGICAL OR PHYSICAL, IN YOUR COMPANY

42 Fear is an Abomination as a Management Tool

Over the last decades we have been subjected to a lot of fashionable theories on people management. One of the more unpleasant theories propagated went like this. If you have 100 people making 100 items and you fired 30 of those 100, the 70 people who remained would be so galvanised by the thought of unemployment they would cover the shortfall by making 100 items between them – fewer people meaning higher productivity per head. The truth of the matter was that in most instances 70 people didn't make 100 items; at times they didn't even make 70. Why? Because very simply most of the time fear doesn't motivate – it paralyses.

Another example of this form of management was Jack Welch, the famous head of General Electric. It was reported he had a view that every year he would cull 10 per cent of his workforce. The judgement as to whom would be in this 10 per cent would be based on a series of KPIs. He argued that people would achieve all those critical indicators based on fear of being in the bottom strata of the company. There is no arguing that GE was successful and I am sure many people would argue that the 'bottom 10 per cent cull' was part of this. However, I think the truth of the situation is that many people were not as productive as they might have been, because of the lurking fear of being a 10 per center.

As employers we should be contributing to people's lives rather than creating further uncertainty. Someone who wakes up in the morning looking forward to going to work will produce a lot more than someone who wakes up in trepidation.

NOBODY DESERVES TO
BE AFRAID AT WORK

43 A Great Thought from a Cleric

Chief Rabbi Jonathan Sacks once spoke at a meeting of The Thirty Club, a gathering of the great and good in communications, which took place over dinner at Claridge's. Several things he said had a really profound effect on me but the most moving quote of all was his belief that, 'Everybody has the right to equal access to hope.'

**TRUE EQUALITY MEANS
EQUAL ACCESS TO HOPE**

44 The Menu Principle of Management

When the creative superstar, David Abbott, joined our tiny agency both Adrian Vickers and I felt a real sense of responsibility because he could literally have gone anywhere. So I determined that I would earn his trust by adopting what I subsequently called the 'Menu Principle of Management'. I would go to his office two or three times a day and run through all the issues that were of concern that day, which were mainly housekeeping. After a while he suggested that he didn't need to be involved in half of the things on the menu. Later during our relationship, that became 80 per cent of the menu which he was happy to leave to me. Finally, the decisions we made were effortless.

He trusted me to understand his attitude towards most of the decisions I took because I learned instinctively how he would react. It made day-to-day life in the agency very easy and enabled David to spend as much time as possible on what he did better than anyone else – great creative work, and participating in the big, important decisions.

MAKE SURE THAT COMMUNICATION IS FREQUENT, DEEP AND WIDESPREAD

45 Never Be a Shouter

When people make a mistake, they know they've made a mistake. When they have to face their boss and discuss the consequences of that mistake, they are already embarrassed and sorry. They feel guilty and are anxious to put the mistake behind them. They also feel that they've let their boss down and are eager to make amends.

If the response from the boss is sympathetic and all about putting the mistake right and making sure it doesn't happen again, then the guilt for making the mistake and the relief that it's been greeted in the right fashion intensifies the desire to get it right next time. We have to assume that someone didn't want to get it wrong and so by definition it was an accident.

If that understanding is not there and the person who made the mistake is shouted at and demeaned then the guilt and absolute desire never to repeat the mistake is replaced by anger. So in many ways the consequences of the mistake are exacerbated.

In these situations understanding is an infinitely better management tool than condemnation.

**COMPASSION IN THE FACE OF MISTAKES
WILL MOST TIMES BE REWARDED**

46 Consistency in Management

The Russian physiologist Ivan Pavlov famously ran a series of experiments using dogs in which he proved that it is possible to condition living creatures' responses to certain things. Pavlov managed to get his dogs to react to the ringing of a bell or another noise as if it were food – the dogs would hear the noise and start salivating even when there was no food presented. At those moments, they would naturally be rather confused and upset, and I expect that the more often this happened, the more unpleasant it became for them because they had no idea what the bell would represent.

My point is that all living things look for consistency – if every time the bell rang the dogs knew they were not going to be fed, they would accept their fate. The inconsistency made the dogs' lives far too complicated for them to be happy.

I'm not suggesting that anybody in management anywhere intentionally runs their business using these techniques. However, quite often there is a great deal of inconsistency. You can create a dispirited workforce very rapidly if your responses to situations become erratic and unpredictable.

**MAKE SURE YOU MANAGE
CONSISTENTLY BUT NOT PREDICTABLY**

47 Bending the Truth

There are an increasing number of people who outline a fictional version of events and then a short time later convince themselves those events really did take place. These are very dangerous people to deal with because they have a complete belief that the lie they knowingly told in the first place has suddenly become the absolute truth. This mode of behaviour was heavily featured in a celebrated biography and labelled as 'reality distortion'. It is very difficult for employees to work for managers who they know are guilty of bending the truth.

NEVER REINVENT THE PAST OR BELIEVE ALTERNATIVE TRUTHS

48 Resentment, the Most Insidious Relationship Killer

Resentment is a very dangerous emotion. If not treated quickly, it can destroy relationships. The biggest problem with resentment comes when it exists on both sides of an argument, when each side quite often has a kernel of justification for their feeling.

During the last recession, I heard of a story involving a client and an advertising agency. The marketing director had been instructed by his board to pull his whole advertising budget for an unspecified period. He fought very hard and managed to get 25 per cent of the budget reinstated. The agency, which was counting on a spend of £8 million, was faced, in the short term, with a £6 million shortfall. They deeply resented the fact that they were faced with difficult decisions internally over the reduced budget. The client had put his job on the line to argue for the £2 million spend and resented the fact that the agency did not understand the possible career threatening consequences for him.

After a number of very testy meetings and exchanges, a really healthy and productive relationship came to be terminated. Months later, when emotions had settled down, both recognised the extent and the validity of the resentment on the other side but by then it was too late.

LEARN TO SPOT POTENTIAL RESENTMENT AND STOP ITS DEVELOPMENT IMMEDIATELY

49 Don't Let People Become a Flexible Overhead

Sometime early in the 1990s it became very fashionable for public companies to announce to the world that their staff had become a 'flexible overhead'. It was argued that in the event of a downturn in company profits, revenue could always be swelled by taking people costs out of the profit and loss statement. We always found this view abhorrent.

I remember hearing a story about a senior man at another agency who, having been promoted way beyond his capabilities, was told on a Friday afternoon that after 15 years his services were no longer required. He decided not to tell his family of his plight at the traditional Friday evening dinner where they all gathered. He argued that he didn't want to spoil the occasion and might not even tell anybody until Sunday evening so as not to ruin their weekends. But he found himself incapable of carrying this out, told everybody at the Friday dinner and said, 'We all sobbed together.' We determined that wherever we could, we would not be a party to destroying people's lives in this fashion.

Every year just before Christmas we had a party for everybody's families. The first year this took place I dressed up as Father Christmas. I was to make a dramatic entrance into the atrium on the ground floor using the glass wall climber lift. Shortly before my descent, David and I stood on the sixth floor peering down at the excited faces of the waiting kids. David said quietly that if ever we thought about playing ducks and drakes with people's lives we should remind ourselves of those children gazing expectantly up at us. Those were innocent lives we had no right to disturb.

Of course, I am talking about much easier times. The tyranny of 90-day results reporting and the seemingly endless assault on margins has greatly increased pressure on the modern manager. But the principle remains the same.

REMEMBER YOUR ROLE IN YOUR EMPLOYEES' LIVES

THEM AND US

In my early days in the ad business, I worked for S. H. Benson, one of the big, venerable agencies dating back to 1893. The board were godlike figures who were never around after lunch as they had decamped to their personal bar for the rest of their day after their full meal. They were rarely seen on any of the working floors. I assumed that these gods maintained top-level contact with the agency's biggest clients but to us mere mortals there was no real indication of this. Indeed, if you were in a relatively full lift on the ground floor of Benson's offices – at 129 Kingsway in London – and the chairman approached, everybody had to leave the lift so he could travel up in splendid isolation. It was rumoured that on the short walk from his apartment in Russell Square to the office he did *The Times* crossword in his head.

The problem we employees faced at Benson's was that if you were bad at your job nobody noticed but, frustratingly, if you were any good you didn't come to anybody's attention either. I thought I'd done a pretty decent job in the marketing department but it wasn't at the cutting edge of the agency. Because the creative process was not at the heart of everything the agency did, power resided with the account men, who controlled the agency's relationships with its clients. The role of account men can be neatly summed up as representatives of the agency to the client and representatives of the client to the agency. I had already spent the early part of my career working on accounts in the international department and decided that was the role that I enjoyed most. In a rather desultory way I started to think about my future and decided to apply for a transfer back into account handling.

Around this time a couple of major clients fired the agency. This was a very nasty wake-up call for the board. After a root and branch review of all their staff resources, they concluded that they had too many account men, some of whom should be culled, together with a number of the ageing creative people. Having announced that I didn't want to be in the marketing department but wanted to be an account man, I was a classic and irresistible candidate for redundancy. There was a day of the long knives at 129 where for the first time in its history Benson's 'let people go'. I was the first, joined later in the day by a lady called Helen Bonington, the mother of the soon-to-be world-famous mountaineer Chris Bonington. I can't remember who got rid of me but I know that Helen was fired by the hawkish head of copy. She responded to the shock of hearing that her services were to be dispensed with by hitting him with her handbag!

50 Cost Cutting, the Modern Panacea

Almost everything that is written about companies these days is fuelled by an obsession with discussions about costs. Costs have to be slashed, we are told. People have to get used to earning less money. People have to work harder. And most of all we are told that fewer people have to be used. The modern Grail is to be the lowest cost producer through huge investment in procurement departments.

I would argue that this view attacks the problem from the wrong end. As I have explained earlier, well-motivated, secure, valued people working for you will achieve productivity levels which are often astonishing. The truth is you only need four well-motivated, secure, valued employees to achieve what eight insecure, frightened employees will achieve. The net result is the same – you will produce more with fewer people, but the upside is enormous. And there is no downside.

In a similar vein, this is also true of taking value out of products: reducing the offering for the same price; using answering machines instead of people; cramming more seats into the same space on planes, boats and trains as people get bigger. How silly is that?

**GETTING MORE FOR LESS
IS NOT SUSTAINABLE**

51 Increasing Revenue Versus Cutting Costs

Increasing revenue is light years more effective at improving a company's health than cutting costs.

In the short-term-focused environment we find ourselves in, cutting costs is often the only option available to beleaguered managers. However, the trouble with cutting costs is that lots of companies cut through the fat into the muscle and the bone, which means it is an act that can't be repeated for more than two or three years or else the company will die.

On the other hand, if the focus is on increasing revenue and that goal is achieved, everybody will feel better. This transmits to potential customers and there is only upside.

**INCREASING REVENUE IS ALWAYS
BETTER THAN CUTTING COSTS**

52 When Making Savings Don't Confuse Cost with Value

There comes a time every so often in a company's life when costs should be reviewed. This is particularly appropriate when jobs are under threat. It happened to us at the end of the 80s, a time of severe recession. Clients were slashing their expenditure and we had to take a good long look at all our ancillary costs to see if savings could be made to protect our workforce.

In the early days of the agency we had a breakfast bar which doubled up as a subsidised bar in the evenings. The concept was really quite simple: if anybody arrived before nine o'clock they got a free breakfast and in the evenings, the bar sold beer more cheaply than any pub in the vicinity. During the quest for austerity our Deputy CFO came to me and said that he had worked out a way of saving £15,000 a year. He then went on to say rather triumphantly that if we closed the bar we would make this relatively significant saving.

What he failed to understand, until I gently explained it to him, was that by getting people to work early in the morning, making them happy with a free breakfast and then helping to develop relationships in the evening, the bar was infinitely more valuable than the sum he had named. The value of a fully motivated workforce is not worth putting at risk for minor savings.

BE CLEAR ABOUT THE DIFFERENCE BETWEEN COST AND VALUE

53 The Ripple Effect

There is a macho belief that decision-making is all and the great managers are separated from their inferior fellows by their ability to make decisions. This is partly true, but here are some words of caution.

Making a decision is in itself only the start of the process, because the decision then has to be managed. Any major decision will have reverberations and any manager worth their salt will clearly understand those reverberations before they make, or at least before they announce, their decision.

It's what I like to call the ripple effect of management. It is like dropping a large stone into a pond – you can be absolutely certain where the main splash is going to occur, but you had better know where the ripples from dropping the stone finish. If not, you will find that the banks of your pond could be irretrievably damaged by those ripples' effects.

The effects of poorly thought-out decisions could be equally catastrophic in your organisation. The words 'I never thought of that' should rarely, if ever, be used by a great manager.

UNDERSTANDING THE CONSEQUENCES OF A DECISION BEFORE IT IS IMPLEMENTED IS CRITICAL

54 Confusing Activity with Progress

In the last few years, I have used this expression more and more and it seems increasingly appropriate to the age we live in. People seem to think there is an urgent need to demonstrate activity, which they believe is a way of justifying a business existence. The truth is we are becoming swamped by increasingly pointless activity that not only leads nowhere but in some cases is positively dangerous.

Take the example of 'smart motorways'. We were told that these would be the safest roads in the country, and that they would ensure the traffic moved faster and more efficiently. They are based on eliminating the 'hard shoulder', the lane where vehicles can stop if they break down for any reason – the premise being that, as long as there is a space to pull in every one and a half miles, the hard shoulder could be used much more effectively as an extra lane.

But the reality is that, despite enormous expense and disruption, smart motorways have been demonstrated to be neither smart nor safe, as coroner's inquests into the victims of the disappearance of hard shoulders have shown. Vehicles are patently not always able to reach the one and a half mile distanced laybys every time they break down. It is a classic case of confusing activity with progress.

We waste an enormous amount of time and energy on activity which, unless it leads to progress, has no value at all. We should ask ourselves as we finish our next meeting what it has achieved apart from deciding the date of a subsequent meeting.

ACTIVITY WHICH DOES NOT LEAD TO PROGRESS HAS NO VALUE

55 Tenacity is a Management Tool

The lazy approach to management is a shrugging of the shoulders and acceptance of inevitability. For a long time at AMV we had a belief that we should never re-pitch for a piece of business we already had. We argued that the chances of winning the re-pitch were remote and we wanted to avoid a double hit on staff morale.

This seemed sensible and was the operating norm for a number of years. Its demise coincided with the appointment of a new head of the company, Farah Ramzan Golant. She was appointed just as three incredibly important clients announced a review of their business and invited her and the agency to participate in a re-pitch. She could have stuck to our belief that re-pitching was a waste of time, the agency would have shrunk overnight, and jobs would have been at threat. However, the fearsomely bright, energetic but above all tenacious Farah thought she could win each of the three re-pitches, and she did. The outlook for the company was transformed by her attitude. She was right and I was wrong.

TENACITY IS A SERIOUSLY UNDERRATED MANAGEMENT TOOL

56 The Value of Time

From the early days, we had a rule that the agency would always close at one p.m. on the Friday before any bank holiday. This would enable our people to get away a bit early and avoid the horrendous traffic jams that occurred just prior to any holiday weekend. We always added the proviso that clients still had to be serviced and invariably found that people who had work to do would waive the right to this extra half day.

One of the companies we acquired heard about this procedure and followed my insistence that it should be applied to their staff as well. They then rang me and said that they had run a spread sheet outlining how much complying with my request was going to cost in lost productivity. They, of course, had not taken into account the goodwill that this gesture generated and I argued persuasively and insistently that this goodwill was vastly more valuable in the quest for greater productivity than any of the costs that they had calculated.

I'm convinced that these gestures contributed enormously to us having the lowest number of people per million pounds billing for most of the life of the agency.

**OFTEN THE BEST BONUS
OF ALL IS THE GIFT OF TIME**

57 How to Write

One of the biggest issues in business today is the lack of clear communication that usually comes down to people hiding behind emails or online messaging (memos in my day were the nearest equivalent). If you must communicate this way, and sometimes in a big company it's essential, it must be done correctly.

The great David Ogilvy sent out a note on September 7th, 1982, directing it to everyone employed at Ogilvy & Mather, the respected ad agency he'd founded more than 30 years before. The memo was entitled 'How to Write'.

> *The better you write, the higher you go in Ogilvy & Mather.*
> *People who think well, write well.*
>
> *Woolly minded people write woolly memos, woolly letters and woolly speeches.*
>
> *Good writing is not a natural gift. You have to learn to write well. Here are 10 hints:*
>
> 1. *Read* Writing that Works: How to Communicate Effectively in Business *by Kenneth Roman and Joel Raphaelson. Read it three times.*
> 2. *Write the way you talk. Naturally.*

3. Use short words, short sentences and short paragraphs.
4. Never use jargon words like reconceptualise, demassification, attitudinally, judgmentally. They are hallmarks of a pretentious ass.
5. Never write more than two pages on any subject.
6. Check your quotations.
7. Never send a letter or a memo on the day you write it. Read it aloud the next morning – and then edit it.
8. If it is something important, get a colleague to improve it.
9. Before you send your letter or your memo, make sure it is crystal clear what you want the recipient to do.
10. If you want ACTION, don't write. Go and tell the guy what you want.

Several decades since David wrote those words they are, if anything, more appropriate than ever.

WRITTEN COMMUNICATION COMPANY-WIDE SHOULD BE CLEAR, CONCISE, OCCASIONALLY INSPIRATIONAL AND ALWAYS RELEVANT

58 Attend to Your Business the Connaught Way

In the years before AMV merged with BBDO, Marvin Sloves, our then US partner, rang me one day and asked if I would meet the deal broker of a very good US agency. As was my habit, I arranged a meeting over breakfast at The Connaught Hotel in Carlos Place, which runs between two of London's power squares, Grosvenor and Berkeley.

Throughout most of the 80s, and a good proportion of the 90s, I would breakfast there at least three days a week. Breakfast was a pretty formal affair and the staff were a well-oiled machine, dispensing the best bacon, tomato and sausage in town, overseen by a maître d' dressed in full evening wear.

Following Marvin's request, I arrived to meet with Susan Smith, who was very high up in the Boston advertising agency Hill Holiday. The breakfast was to be our first exploratory meeting to see if there was any basis on which we could acquire the Boston agency, which was known for its high level of creativity.

As I walked in I was told that my guest had already arrived and was at my normal table. While I was making my way across the dining room, the maître d' gave me a note which read, 'Your flies are undone'. Having introduced myself to Susan, I explained to her that there was, what is now fashionably called, a 'wardrobe malfunction' and she should avert her gaze while I corrected it.

Having made my trousers whole again we had a very pleasant breakfast, laughed about my open flies and left promising to meet again soon. A concerned waiter stopped me on the way out asking if my trousers were all right because, if not, they had a valet standing by with a dressing gown so that one of their tailors could repair the zip. Service from a bygone age!

ALWAYS EXCEED YOUR
CLIENTS' EXPECTATIONS

59 Every Business is Detail

John Sainsbury famously said, 'Retail is detail'. The truth of the matter is that every business is detail. Once you have established your business's principles and beliefs and established the matrix around them, you have to worry about them on a daily basis. Every little decision you make must be judged against that behavioural matrix.

A company culture takes an enormous amount of time to develop and unless it is nourished and kept constantly in view, it will disappear through your fingers like fine sand.

JUDGE EVERY DECISION AGAINST YOUR COMPANY'S PRINCIPLES AND BELIEFS

60 Let's Do it for Cav

I began to take an interest in the Tour de France after my son explained to me the mysteries of the Peloton. I was enthralled by the majesty of the event, but my overwhelming feeling was of admiration for the teamwork and selflessness of the best teams.

During the 2012 race, management for the British team suggested that Bradley Wiggins, their race leader, should be nursed through two stages. He responded that was unacceptable and that he and the rest of the team wanted to make sure another member, Mark Cavendish, could win a further sprint stage in addition to the one he had already won. All of them pushed themselves to the limit to ensure Cavendish was positioned to win at the appropriate time. This subjugation of personal egos and ambition for the good of the team was breathtaking.

It's not only business that can learn from this. I'm reminded of JFK's inaugural speech when he urged people to ask not what their country could do for them but what they could do for their country. If we could foster this thought in our businesses and, probably more importantly, in our society then we would be in much better shape.

**UNDERSTAND THAT EVERY SO OFTEN
INDIVIDUAL REQUIREMENTS CAN BE
CRITICAL FOR THE GOOD OF THE WHOLE**

61 Another Night at the Grosvenor House Hotel

AMV has been very fortunate to win a number of awards which are usually given out during a slightly drunken evening in the Great Room at The Grosvenor House Hotel. One year the host for the evening was Jimmy Tarbuck, who had become an acquaintance of mine. He introduced me as 'living proof that Snow White and Dopey had sex' – as far as I was concerned too many people laughed out loud for comfort.

But there is a serious point to make about awards and particularly those creative ones that are judged by other creatives from across the spectrum of agencies. It's a lovely experience to stand up and receive an award for a particular piece of work, but the real benefit is that the more awards we won, the more the very best creative people wanted to work for us. It is said that clients pooh-pooh the industry's award structure but over the last 20 years many clients I have shared a table with have been just as excited that our work – and their brand – was being recognised.

However, the best award in the agency's history had nothing to do with a trip to Grosvenor House. This award was a US import. For many years in the States, the 'Hundred Best Companies to Work For' award was the annual accolade that all companies strove for. The mechanism was simple – the company compiling the awards would request complete access to every member of staff and then ask them to fill in a questionnaire based on a well-researched set of criteria establishing what made a company a good place to work. All employees and their comments remained anonymous.

The award came to the UK and, along with hundreds of other companies, we were asked to participate. The scheme over here was run by *The Sunday Times* and the publication of the results was eagerly awaited. In the awards' inaugural year AMV was voted the seventh best company in the UK to work for. We were way ahead of any other company in our business and this was a source of great pride to us all because it was our employees who had voted for us.

Here's a word of warning for those people who don't take enough care to understand the implications of this award. A couple of years ago a major operation in the UK decided that it would be a good idea to enter. Not only did it not win a place in the top 100 but the feedback from staff demonstrated that it would have been a prime candidate for one of the 100 worst companies to work for. The results demonstrated an astonishing lack of connection with the company's staff and an inability to understand how badly management was failing.

**ENTER AWARD SCHEMES – WINNING
PLACES A SPRING IN EVERYONE'S STEP**

62 I'm Sorry We've Made a Mistake

The very best companies quite often are defined by the way they handle mistakes, complaints or deficiencies in their product offering. I've recently had the experience of trying to get an expensive Swiss watch serviced only to find it has to be sent back to Switzerland. The process could take months and it might result in a hefty bill which would add insult to injury.

In contrast, a little while ago a product made by a manufacturer called Bowers & Wilkins – an iPod dock with a speaker and amplifier called a Zeppelin Air – that I had purchased some years before developed a fault. There was no question that its warranty had expired and there was more than a hint that I might have been responsible for the malfunction.

When we telephoned them to explain the fault and ask for guidance, they could not have been more helpful. They sent us transit packaging so we could return the product to them and within two weeks of receiving the errant item they repaired the fault and serviced the rest of the machine. It was returned completely free of charge with a letter of apology from a senior person at Bowers & Wilkins. A really classy company behaving in a high-class way.

UNDERSTAND THAT THE RESPONSE TO A MISTAKE IS MUCH MORE IMPORTANT THAN THE INFRACTION ITSELF

4

LEADERSHIP

63 The Difference Between Leaders and Managers

Leaders are people who tap into the human psyche and motivate and inspire it; managers use that inspiration to run efficient, decent and consequently profitable businesses.

If you ever discover the very rare individuals who can fill both functions, you must protect them, cherish them and keep them at all costs.

UNDERSTANDING THE DIFFERENCE BETWEEN LEADERSHIP AND MANAGEMENT IS CRUCIAL TO A SUCCESSFUL BUSINESS

64 The Responsibilities of Power

Never ever do things just because you can. When you accede to a position of authority, those little indulgences you used to enjoy become unacceptable. Your time is literally no longer your own.

You are in the spotlight and you should be setting standards of behaviour. If people are waiting to see you and you are late, they have no choice but to sit there and wait. It's because you have the power to keep people waiting that you shouldn't and it's because you don't have to explain yourself that you should.

WITH POWER COMES RESPONSIBILITIES

TREAT YOUR WORKFORCE AS IF THEY WERE YOUR FAMILY

A colleague of mine once said that as he left his house in the morning he pulled on his 'office face' and as he drew into his drive in the evening he pulled on his 'home face'. I was astonished by this. I find it difficult enough to live with one persona let alone two. But it is obviously pretty widespread, because if some chief executives behaved at home the way they behave at the office, the NSPCC and most of the social workers in this country would pursue them for cruelty. It is a fact that we allow individuals to get away with reprehensible behaviour during office hours. I believe the same rules that apply to being a good father at home should apply to being a good boss during the day. An abusive boss should be treated every bit as seriously as an abusive parent.

In my third job in advertising, I joined a newly formed advertising agency called KMP. I'd been there around 10 days when David Kingsley – the K – came up to me early one evening and said, 'Look, I've got to go home … now and there's a very important document being produced for a new business meeting. Is there a chance that you could bring a copy of it to my flat when it's ready later this evening?' Being a working class boy with a complete understanding of my place in the overall scheme of things, I said of course.

I arrived at David's apartment just off Hyde Park at around 8 p.m., rang the bell and the door was opened by David in jeans and sweatshirt. It was the first time it ever occurred to me that bosses actually wore jeans and a sweatshirt. I gave him the document and as I turned to go he said to me, 'Have you eaten yet?' I said, 'No, I'll have a meal when I get home.' He responded that he and his wife were having spaghetti bolognese and he was sure they could stretch it to three so why didn't I join them for dinner?

From that moment on there was nothing I wouldn't do for him. That didn't mean that I thought he was an easy touch but I knew he was a human being. During the time I worked for him, David remained an enormous source of inspiration for his intellect, industry and understanding of the human psyche. I would have run through walls for him.

65 Careless Talk Costs Lives

As a manager, or even more importantly as a leader, you are likely to have tens of conversations every week with the people who work for you. It's impossible to remember word for word every one of those conversations but of one thing you can be certain: the person you've had a conversation with will not only remember every single word but the manner in which it is said, from every inflection to your body language.

Be very careful how you dispense information and be doubly careful of any promise you make during these conversations.

A really good memory is an invaluable leadership tool.

TAKE CARE HOW YOU DISPENSE INFORMATION AND ONLY MAKE PROMISES YOU CAN KEEP

66 Comfort of Your Convictions

A little while ago somebody was talking to me about a mutual acquaintance and said the problem with him was that he was a poor decision maker. At that moment the meaning of the expression 'courage of your convictions' became very clear to me. I realised we should say 'the comfort of your convictions' instead.

The truth is if you have convictions, both in the personal and business sense, then those convictions will probably account for 75 per cent of any decision you're likely to make. That way you're only exercising judgement over 25 per cent of any decision you take and that is a great comfort.

If, on the other hand, you have no convictions, you have to use judgement to account for 100 per cent of any decision. That is both tiring and dangerous and some of the time will definitely end in tears.

I remember having lunch with the famous editor of a Sunday newspaper soon after the New Labour revolution happened. I said to him over coffee that I was concerned I didn't know what Tony Blair stood for. He responded by saying that he had a much greater concern than that. He didn't think Tony Blair knew what Tony Blair stood for.

MAKE SURE THAT CONVICTIONS ARE AT THE HEART OF YOUR DECISION-MAKING

67 Democracy Is No Way to Run a Company

When I set up my first agency at the age of 31, I decided that two things should happen. Firstly, I would have the biggest slug of equity, 33 per cent (justified because I'd raised all the money from two wonderfully supportive people) and I would distribute the rest equally among the four partners I'd persuaded to join me in this venture. At the same time, I told them we would have a different structure to other agencies and we wouldn't have titles. Every decision we made would be a democratic one decided by the five of us. There would be no boss – we would all be the bosses. We initially even toyed with all our names being in the title – until we discovered that Byfield Mead Cruttenden Osborne Whelan was more than our poor, unfortunate receptionist would be able to manage as she answered the phone a hundred times a day.

My idea of trying to impose democracy forced people who wanted to be led into trying to be managers. And it didn't work. Within three years those four people that I'd gifted with equity decided that they could dispense with my services. They came to my flat very early one morning and asked me to leave. A very successful fledgling agency withered and disappeared within 10 years, a victim of a lack of clear management structure and an absence of clearly defined responsibilities.

TEMPTING AS IT MAY SEEM, DEMOCRACY IS NO WAY TO RUN A COMPANY

68 If You're Paid to Do So, Make Sure You Assume Responsibility

In the early days of my first agency, one of our clients was the Milton Keynes Development Corporation. Every Monday there was a gathering of the heads of department to discuss issues of the moment.

I remember one particular meeting when the great CEO Fred Lloyd Roche threw open a particularly knotty problem to the assembled forum. One by one everybody was allowed to express an opinion. When we were all finished, Fred thanked us and made to move on to the next item on the agenda.

The chief architectural officer interrupted this move by asking if we were going to vote on the point we had just discussed. Fred asked why he thought he was part of a democratic process. Of course we wouldn't vote on it, Fred said. Having solicited all opinions, Fred himself would make the decision. This might be affected by what the others had said but Fred was paid to decide the next move forward and that's precisely what he did.

Management by committee doesn't work. In most instances the buck should stop with the guy who earns the most bucks.

**ASSUME THE RESPONSIBILITIES
THAT YOU ARE PAID TO ASSUME**

69 Relationships, Relationships, Relationships

In business, and probably in life, there are only three things that are important: relationships, relationships, relationships. It doesn't matter how smart or how good you are, if you can't develop relationships you will make little progress either personally or professionally, nor can you create a valuable business. And it doesn't matter if you are manufacturing ball bearings or running an advertising agency.

When we decided that AMV needed outside investment an offer for sale document was created. The introduction to that document laid down a combination of beliefs, operating principles and behavioural principles which formed the bedrock for the ongoing relationships that we wanted to create with our investors. This document was also seen by our clients and, importantly our people, and the words we used were a reaffirmation of our commitment to the relationships that would define our future involvement together. It read as follows:

i. The agency began with a set of beliefs that are still the cornerstone of the way in which it operates and that are, therefore, as relevant to its future prospects as they are to its past performance.

ii. The principal requirement of clients from agencies is outstanding creative work. Hence all our structures and disciplines are designed to reflect the fact that the creative function is the most important part of our business.

iii. Our clients place great trust in us. We spend large sums on their behalf. We are honest in our advice, even when it does not serve our own short-term interests. This earns respect and creates long-term relationships.

iv. We value our skills and the service we give. We work with small growth companies as well as major clients, but we expect a fair return.

v. The agency is an agreeable, fair and humane place in which to work. In an industry characterised by a high turnover of staff, the way to retain people is to keep them happy.

vi. Success brings responsibilities as well as rewards. The advertising we produce is in the public eye and is always good mannered and truthful. We will not create advertising we would not want our own families to see.

Around that time MORI, a respected polling company, conducted a survey of 176 marketing directors about advertising agencies. Their conclusions noted that AMV 'really does seem to be in some way unique and different from all other agencies'.

GOOD RELATIONSHIPS ARE AT THE HEART OF ANY SUCCESSFUL BUSINESS

70 Feared, Loved or Respected?

There has been a live debate since commerce began about which of these descriptors is most desirable in a successful business leader. I remember reading about a new chief executive at one of the world's biggest corporations. It was said of him that 'he was a brutal man of limited tastes'. His tenure of office was neither successful nor prolonged. He was succeeded by a much gentler man who was tagged as being really nice but not decisive. Not surprisingly, his appointment didn't work out either. Neither of these men were successful, because they didn't possess the most significant attribute – the ability to command respect.

The world is littered with tough men who were relentless in their pursuit of success. The late Steve Jobs of Apple was a classic example – a man who, it is said, would put aside the niceties of relationships for the sake of his business. I'm sure that the people who worked for him would express an element of fear of him as an individual but at the same time enormous respect for his crusade for perfection. Less talented or driven individuals than Mr Jobs should adopt his management style at their peril. Fear coupled with respect works only as long as things go swimmingly. If there is a downturn, these people have no reservoir of goodwill (something I believe affection creates) to see them through rocky patches.

Obviously the most important of the three descriptors is 'respected'. I've always believed that this characteristic, coupled with being liked by the people who work for you, is much more important and long-lasting than the energy and ultimate paralysis that fear engenders. Respect should be earned before it can be commanded. Being given the benefit of the doubt from an early stage, through the use of affection as opposed to fear, makes that mission a lot easier.

ACHIEVING RESPECT AND AFFECTION MAKES LEADERSHIP MUCH EASIER

71 Micro and Macro Management

My fervent belief is that having appointed managers, my role was to let them manage. By definition, management is a succession of small decisions – really large ones rarely happen – and if you can't trust your people to handle the day-to-day then they shouldn't be in place.

Empower your managers to deliver and if they don't deliver, replace them. Micro-management will suffocate them and will quite often lead to formulaic lowest common denominator yardsticks. If this is your management belief, in the years to come you will be employing programmable robots to carry out your instructions. The best leaders never micro-manage and above all are never afraid of employing people better than themselves. The really great ones lead themselves out of a job.

NEVER BE A MICROMANAGER AND ALWAYS EMPLOY PEOPLE WHO ARE BETTER THAN YOU

72 Find a Fearless Finance Director

Far too many businesses set up by strong-minded, strong-willed and overly confident entrepreneurs ignore this. We found such a man, who is sadly no longer with us. James McDanell wasn't afraid of me, he wasn't afraid of David Abbott and he wasn't afraid of Adrian Vickers. He had complete confidence in his professional ability and as a result told us the unvarnished truth the whole time. He said to me at our first interview, when I baulked at how expensive I thought he would be, that if he couldn't make that much difference legitimately – i.e. cover his salary – within two months of joining us, then we should fire him.

He transformed our business. His presence meant that we could all get on with doing our day jobs – the jobs that we were good at. David could write ads, Adrian and I could look after clients and James, who we could trust with our lives, made sure that the money took care of itself. It was an enormous liberation to have James and a tragedy that he died so young. Above all he believed in doing the right thing – he never talked about financial engineering or pushing the edge of the envelope. He was just the safest of a safe pair of hands. We could all sleep soundly at night.

AS SOON AS YOU CAN AFFORD IT, FIND A FINANCE DIRECTOR WHO ISN'T AFRAID OF YOU

73 The Myth of the 'Mission Statement'

People spend hours, days and sometimes years, putting together a 'Mission Statement'. I have sat in meetings where we've argued interminably about the meaning of a single word in a Mission Statement. What normally happens is the process of producing the Statement is so agonising that once it's written everybody breathes a heavy sigh of relief and thinks the job is done. In reality it's only just started – it's the Mission that's important and not the Statement. Walking the walk is infinitely more critical to a business than talking the talk.

The story goes that when the Creative Artists Agency was started in Los Angeles in 1975 – by Steve Ovitz, Ron Meyer, Mike Rosenfeld and others – they wanted to create a business that was as simple as the company they were leaving, William Morris, was complex. There was no agonising over what they wanted to be in their Mission Statement. What they put on the wall of their first office in Century City was just: 'Be a team player' and 'Return phone calls promptly'.

How positive and inclusive is that.

**WALKING THE WALK IS MORE
IMPORTANT THAN TALKING THE TALK**

74 Politics, the Cancer of Business

There is scarcely a company in the universe that doesn't have politics operating within it. I guess it is impossible to eradicate politics completely, but as I have suggested in the heading, it is a cancer that can destroy companies. This is the root cause of trouble in business and countless non-productive hours are spent by people at every level in company politicking.

Politics thrives in an environment caused by a vacuum. A vacuum created by indecision, weak management and a lack of direction. That's the key point: politics in business is, by and large, the fault of business managers and not of the people who indulge in politics.

Politics can be avoided by strong leaders who make and manage decisions and lay down a behavioural matrix for the company that all employees of that company can participate in and subscribe to. There are very few people who enjoy politics in their company. Quite often it's a product of despair and frustration, and it must be largely eradicated for any company to be successful long term.

DEVELOP AN ABILITY TO SPOT EARLY SIGNS OF COMPANY POLITICS AND STOP THEM AT SOURCE

75 Don't Be Beguiled by Flattery

Once you start believing your own publicity and embracing stuff that is written about you as the truth, then you are in trouble. There is a chance you will start behaving in a way that is driven by those outside perceptions rather than reality. I would argue that many of the more sensational failings in business were contributed to by people being seduced by what the world was saying about them.

The very best leaders retain a healthy level of scepticism and insecurity about themselves. This results in them constantly evaluating their achievements through honest eyes rather than through the inevitably superficial and ill-informed view that the rest of the world propagates about them.

**A REASONABLE LEVEL OF SELF-DOUBT
IS GREAT FOR MOTIVATION**

76 How to Discover the Real Truth

The problem with being at the top, or near the top, of any organisation is that people try to guess what it is they think you want to hear and tell you that, as opposed to simply telling you what you need to hear.

Learn to listen to really junior members of the organisation, the ones who work at the coalface. As long as their anonymity is respected and they're not placed in a compromising situation, they can be sources of information that is critical to the health of the company.

Recently I've had experience of an individual who revels in a reputation as a really nice person. However, any really junior employee quizzed about him will suggest that his niceness is only skin deep – a weapon to be used for personal benefit. This person's pleasantness does not extend much past people who can be of immediate use.

**KEEP YOUR EARS VERY
CLOSE TO THE GROUND**

77 How to Be a Boss and a Human Being at the Same Time

On days when I don't have a business lunch, I make a point of getting my own sandwiches. Before my trip to the local sandwich bar I ask if I can get anything for anybody else. There is nothing particularly special about this, in my view. I've always thought it was totally unacceptable that I would ask somebody to go and get me my sandwiches in their lunch hour. They would have to bite into their precious free time just to make sure that I was fed.

On many occasions travelling on British Airways, the more mature airline staff would tell me about the days when Lord King and Lord Marshall ran the business. They told me stories of how Colin Marshall would roll up his sleeves and help get passenger food ready in the galley once the plane was in the air. One of them told me proudly of the time that Colin spotted that a door was slightly loose, found a screwdriver and repaired it. His presence and charisma underlined the fact that he was the boss but his ability to get stuck in and help out meant that the people who worked at BA would follow his lead anywhere.

GREAT LEADERS RETAIN THE COMMON TOUCH

78 The Illusion of Involvement

There comes a time in everybody's business life when they have to move on, either upwards or sideways. From personal experience, I know this to be a very difficult time – handing over executive power and corporate responsibility is tough. But it has to be done cleanly, positively and without any room for doubt.

If the inheritor of the power is a sensitive individual, they will make the transition period less brutal by including the previous holder on emails. But while there are undoubtedly things that the passer of the flame can be useful on, to give them the belief they still have the power to alter decisions (when they no longer do) is not only unhelpful, it could be argued to be cruel.

Once the power has passed on, the belief that involvement is still at the highest level and can be exercised should be resisted at all costs.

**SUCCESSION WORKS BEST
WHEN IMPLEMENTED CLEANLY**

79 Should We Reward Job Creators or Job Destroyers?

A few years ago I was fortunate enough to be playing golf on one of Scotland's great courses, Carnoustie. Because of my lack of both talent and knowledge, I would always have a caddie with me as I tried to navigate my way around this beautiful torture chamber.

As we walked I asked my wonderfully patient, newly acquired friend how long he had been a guide around the bunkers and heather there. He told me that he had been doing the job for around four years. I asked him what he had done before and he said he had been a middle manager in one of Scotland's biggest banks for 25 years.

He went on to say that one Friday four years earlier, after he returned from lunch, he was given a black plastic bag and told to clear his desk that afternoon. He was escorted off the premises by a security guard and never returned. I asked him how he'd managed to cope. He said that he hadn't and still took Prozac every day.

Fred Goodwin (ex 'Sir'), the prime architect of the temporary destruction of my caddie's life, was subsequently given one of the highest honours this country can bestow. Before the inevitable demise of the 'great man', he had a reputation for being one of the great destroyers of people's hopes and dreams.

Surely common humanity and good business sense suggest that every person who manages other people should be rewarded for satisfying and helping to fulfil hopes and dreams, and not for destroying them?

IT MAKES BETTER BUSINESS SENSE TO CREATE JOBS THAN DESTROY THEM

80 Leaders and Managers – the Elusive Blend

Many companies go through a period when managers try to be leaders when they're not and never will be. It's particularly evident when dealing with companies that have been set up from scratch by a group of entrepreneurs.

By definition, the next group of people they hire tend to be managers because founders view themselves, quite properly, as leaders. The mix works very well until the time comes for the founders/leaders to retire or leave the company.

It's then left in the hands of the managers, who were selected for management skills rather than leadership skills. It's enormously difficult to teach leadership. While leaders accept that they are not always brilliant managers, managers tend to believe that leadership is an attribute that can be acquired. It can't.

However, I've noticed that the next layer down from those early managers quite often spawns a group of younger people who are restless to go back to the practices and beliefs of the original leaders of the business. These people must be given their head, and more often than not 'leaders' will emerge.

**ALWAYS INCLUDE UNCONVENTIONAL
SOLUTIONS IN DISCUSSIONS ABOUT
MANAGEMENT SUCCESSION**

81 Make Sure Your Company Can Survive Without You

Everyone should be free to choose where they want to work and in good times the market often creates better opportunities elsewhere, which offer the prospect of individual self-advancement. However, I do believe that the very top managers have an obligation outside of the normal parameters.

That obligation means that their freedom to change their career path has to be tempered by their responsibility to the people who work for them in their current role. Before they move on, the absolute imperative is that they have created something that can survive without them, and in some instances indeed flourish with a fresh injection of top management. Until that point is reached, self-interest should be secondary.

At the very highest level, David Cameron owed the United Kingdom rather more as a country than an immediate resignation on the morning after he lost the Brexit vote. As the architect of the situation which led to a victory for the Leavers, the very least he could have done was to stay around and enact the will of the people who he had vowed to serve.

A GOOD LEADER WILL ALWAYS HAVE THEIR REPLACEMENT IN MIND BEFORE MOVING ON

82 Never Lose Your Sense of Wonder

Many years ago a couple of fruit farmers in California were growing pears. They were great pears, juicy and succulent and they gave the farmers, Harry and Fred, a very good living. A trend emerged around Christmas time for people to buy pears as presents. One year a relatively large customer asked if the pears could be boxed to enhance their value as gifts. In the ensuing years, the demand for boxed pears increased enormously and the margins on boxed pears far exceeded those obtainable from normal loose pear sales. Harry and Fred had an increasingly profitable and growing business.

One day they decided they could intensify this growth using advertising. They went to New York hoping to meet advertising's great guru of the time, one Raymond Rubicam. His agency Young & Rubicam was the hottest thing in town. Intrigued by Harry and Fred, he agreed to see them. Sensibly they brought samples along and Raymond thought they were the best pears he'd ever tasted. However, he was concerned that the cost of an advertising campaign might be too high. He suggested that the agency present a media plan before doing any creative work to ensure that the capital cost was acceptable.

Two weeks later another meeting was convened in New York and the media schedule was presented. Top of the list of candidate magazines was probably the most influential business magazine in the world. Fred, wide-eyed with a sense of awe after looking at the schedule, said, 'Imagine Harry and me selling our pears in *Fortune*.'

This little parable has stayed with me throughout my career because it represents a very down-to-earth view of business success. Harry and Fred did not believe their own publicity or ever get above themselves. A sense of wonder makes sure that you're always grounded, grateful and surprised at a level of success.

We use Fred's words often in our business. I remember the time David and I turned up at one of Britain's biggest toiletries manufacturers. We were attending a meeting in the boardroom after they'd appointed us to handle the advertising for two of their major brands. I turned to David and said, 'It's a Harry and me selling our pears in *Fortune* moment.' This attitude meant that we never took anything for granted.

**CHERISH A SENSE OF WONDER
SO YOU REMAIN GROUNDED**

83 How Old is Too Old?

There's an expression which says of young players that 'If you're good enough, you're old enough'. I have always subscribed to this, but with the proviso that experience is a very valuable addition to talent.

As I'm rather ancient myself, I also believe that as a society we discard experienced and talented people far too easily, simply because they've reached a notional age which would suggest they're past it.

People should continue to be judged on their ability to do the job, not their age. I was much comforted recently to read that the new chairman of one of our major financial institutions was well past the age where perceived wisdom suggests he should be put out to grass.

WISDOM BASED ON EXPERIENCE IS A MUCH OVER-LOOKED WEAPON IN MANAGEMENT

5

STRATEGY

84 Biggest or Best?

When we set up Abbott Mead Vickers, we never aspired to be the biggest advertising agency; in fact the possibility never even occurred to us. The only sustainable ambition, in our view, was to want to be the best because that's the thing that keeps you striving day after day after day.

The truth is this restless search and mission to be the best, to our enormous surprise, one day led to Abbott Mead Vickers becoming the biggest. As I said in a memo to everyone at the time, it's amazing how big you can get if you're not worried about how big you can get. That same memo said a big thank you from the acorns to the oak tree.

Steve Jobs was once asked 'is your goal to overtake the PC in market share?' He answered with a smile: 'I can tell you what our goal is; our goal is to make the best personal computers in the world and make products we are proud to sell and would recommend to our family and friends. We don't ship junk.'

IF YOU SET OUT TO BE THE BIGGEST YOU WILL NEVER BE THE BEST. IF YOU WANT TO BE THE BEST THERE IS A REAL CHANCE OF BECOMING THE BIGGEST AS A BY-PRODUCT

85 Profit: Principle or Consequence?

There has always been a belief in our company that if you do good work and look after your people, success and money will follow. It has to be a consequence of what you do and not a principle of it. I assume everyone everywhere would agree with the opening statement. However you will find that most express it as: 'You make money by doing good work and looking after your people.' By looking at it that way you subtly, but importantly, change the principle.

If money is the first thing you think of, then you are bound to compromise on good work and people. Good work and people (in either order) have to come first and second and the consequential success that should follow is both inevitable and deserved. However – and be under no illusion about this – you have to make money doing what you're doing to validate your principles and beliefs.

PROFIT SHOULD ALWAYS BE A CONSEQUENCE RATHER THAN A PRINCIPLE, IF IT IS TO LAST

86 Don't Be Afraid of Your Competitors

The whole world is based on competition in one form or another and it makes a great deal of sense to monitor your competitors' activities. In an ideal world you learn lessons from their mistakes before you make them yourself.

But all too often companies become obsessed with the success that their competitors are enjoying. This obsession can lead to an unhealthy aping of competitive activity, quite often before that activity is deemed a success or failure. I have seen many a marketing plan over the years that might have been written by the marketing director of the competition rather than the company itself.

If you have found a new way of satisfying your customers in your company and its method of operation, build on that. It has been said that business life is about building a better mousetrap, but it might be more sensible to find a way of getting rid of mice completely. Lateral thinking is enormously important and not always obvious. Henry Ford once said if he'd relied on research, he would have spent most of his life trying to breed a faster horse instead of creating a mass-market alternative form of transport.

**WATCH THE COMPETITION
BUT DON'T FOLLOW THEM**

87 A Lesson from Sebastian Coe

From the early days of our company I have used an analogy which involves Sebastian, now Lord, Coe. At the height of his running career he was the consummate athletic figure of his generation. He glided across the track with powerful elegance. But I drew inspiration from the way he won his races rather than how he ran.

At the final bend of the race, Coe was normally in the lead. His competitors would be bunched behind him gathering their strength as they thought he would be vulnerable to attack as the race neared its end – the problem any front runner faces. At the moment he sensed that the competition was about to try to overtake him, Coe had the ability to accelerate again and break both their resistance and their hearts by moving away and winning.

I think this is a really good lesson for companies. Getting in front is one thing. Continuing to accelerate once you're there is the only way of maintaining your pre-eminence.

ALWAYS HAVE SOMETHING IN RESERVE TO BUILD ON A BUSINESS ADVANTAGE

88 The Benefit of the Doubt – a Golden Gift

When the advertising and communication business is working at its very best, it creates for the products or services it represents the golden state of the benefit of the doubt.

We were able to do that in the early days of our work on Volvo, although it must be said we were helped enormously by the cars' performance. If a customer's Volvo wouldn't start in the morning there was an inclination to believe that maybe the atmosphere was damp, such was the aura of reliability we helped to create around the brand. On the other hand, lesser cars with the same problem would be vilified and held totally responsible for the lack of performance.

Be aware, though, that benefit of the doubt is a fragile ally. Once it is proven to be misplaced, all hell can break loose. The sentiment destroyed can lead to a complete revisiting of all occurrences in the past where the benefit of the doubt was given and a very damaging re-evaluation can take place.

**TRUST IN A BRAND IS PRECIOUS
– PROTECT IT AT ALL COSTS**

89 The Message Not the Medium

In the digital age we are told rather pityingly that we are dinosaurs if we don't understand how deeply significant the digital revolution is and how it has transformed all our lives. The depth and importance of this transformation could be discussed at great length but one eternal truth applies. My partner David Abbott once said, 'Crap that travels at the speed of light is still crap when it gets there.'

I would argue that – now more than ever before – the quality and creativity of the messages we expect our consumers to pay attention to has never been more important. It is certainly much more significant than the vehicle that delivers them.

THE MESSAGE WILL ALWAYS BE MORE IMPORTANT THAN THE MEDIUM

GREENS OF BRIGHTON

Greens was a traditional business in the ready-mixed cake baking sector, so we had to take on the might of Sara Lee for market share. The first commercial that was done by David featured almond slices. It was lovingly shot by John Clark and was the forerunner in film technique of the Sainsbury's recipe commercials some years later. Our relationship with Bruce Noble, the managing director of Greens, was like all our most successful ones – based on a genuine respect and affection.

But at one point in the relationship we were having trouble. We had a series of creative ideas turned down – it was proving difficult to make progress. On one of my five daily visits to David's office, he bemoaned the fact that we couldn't appear to get anything through and said he thought we should resign the business. I agreed to make an appointment with Bruce and drove down to Brighton to give him the bad news. I was ushered into Bruce's office and he was as charming as always – until I told him that regrettably we had to resign because of creative differences.

He astonished me by saying that he refused to accept our resignation of the business. This had never happened to me before, although I have to say I wasn't used to telling clients to go elsewhere either. As I was spluttering and stuttering, he asked if David was in the office, I told him I believed he was, and Bruce said that I should return to London with him following closely behind in his car and that the three of us should get together.

Mobile phones had not been invented so it was difficult for me to prime David in advance. When we reached David's office in Babmaes Street, Bruce expressed bewilderment at the decision we should part based on some creative problems that he could sort out in a heartbeat. After pondering on this, David said that he thought I might have been a bit hasty in resigning the business. Over a cup of tea and a shop-bought almond slice, everybody shook hands and Bruce drove back to Brighton.

It was not the first time that the depth of relationship we had created with a client meant we could have what seemed like a terminal disagreement overturned. The result of this particular episode was a further very productive period of doing business together. And it was another illustration of how well David and I dovetailed.

90 First Among Equals

I spent a lot of my early life delivering special letters to the giant Beecham organisation which sprawled across a number of buildings on the Great West Road. Macleans toothpaste was in one building, Lucozade in another and so on. They were, and are, one of the great British advertisers coveted by all advertising agencies as they have consistently spent heavily on marketing over the years and, despite a couple of changes of ownership, they still do today. There came a point in the history of AMV when we were asked to present for some of their brands and it was a seminal moment in my journey from despatch boy to agency principal because we won some of them.

One day early in our relationship, I was having lunch with the marketing director of Beecham when he asked me who were the most important people in our agency. With absolute conviction I said everybody in our agency was important and to choose one group as being more important than others would be invidious. He said that he took the point but could I indulge him with an answer.

I said that if pushed I would choose the creative people. We were a company that made a living out of delivering ideas that changed things. Central to that was the quality of the message we created for our clients. That being the case, the people whose thoughts on a blank sheet of paper ultimately create business for our clients had to be first among equals. They were indeed the geese that laid the golden eggs. It wouldn't matter if everything else we did was perfect. If we couldn't deliver results through our creative work we would not succeed.

UNDERSTAND THE CORE OF YOUR PRODUCT OFFERING AND GIVE IT EVERY CHANCE TO FLOURISH

91 Creativity and Procurement

Sadly over the years, creativity is finding itself more and more commoditised. The true value of the magic of great creativity seems now to come second to its cost.

Can you imagine, for instance, a few centuries ago, the Pope was having a procurement meeting with Michelangelo. It went something like this... 'So, Mike, we have this project that I want you to quote on. It's this big Chapel ceiling that looks a bit dull. The cardinals and I thought that some sort of painting would liven it up. If you're interested perhaps you can send in a quote with your hourly rate and how many hours you think it will take to paint the ceiling. As well, would you estimate the cost of paint and brushes and turps etc. We've also asked eight other painters to quote so it is competitive and cost will be a critical element in deciding who gets the job.'

John Ruskin wrote the following about paying for work:

> 'It's unwise to pay too much, but it's worse to pay too little. When you pay too much you lose a little – that's all. When you pay too little, you sometimes lose everything because the thing you bought was incapable of doing the thing it was bought to do. The common law of business balance prohibits paying a little and getting a lot – it can't be done. If you deal with the lowest bidder, it is well to add

> *something for the risk you run, and if you do that*
> *you will have enough to pay for something better.'*

Over decades the advertising business has not placed enough value on the difference that great creative work can make. Because by and large we operate in unquantifiable arenas, we have not made compelling enough cases linking creativity with effectiveness. The industry governing body IPA, through its Effectiveness Awards, has tried as hard as anybody but the essential link between the two has not been established. The ability to charge a premium for the very best has fallen away and it's our own fault.

YOU SHOULD ALWAYS PAY A PREMIUM FOR THE BEST – THAT INCLUDES CREATIVITY

92 Obligations to Excellence

At one stage in the life of our agency a client, Captain Morgan Rum, was proving very difficult. We had work turned down and the relationship was becoming increasingly fractious. On one of the many occasions that David and I sat over a cup of tea in his office, I suggested the time had come when we should resign the business.

David countered by saying that we had no right to resign because we had not produced good enough work. He agreed that a parting of the ways was almost inevitable but that it shouldn't happen until we produced a campaign that we were really proud of. We would not earn the right to quit until we had satisfied our obligation to do great work.

Soon after that he did produce a great campaign and – surprise, surprise – the relationship with the client got better almost immediately, which meant we didn't have to resign it. It would have been all too easy to take the option of quitting while we were behind.

LIVE UP TO YOUR OWN HIGH STANDARDS

93 The Party and the Balloon

I had a very simple brief for our financial people – it was that everybody had to leave the party with a balloon.

If one of the guys came back and said he had done a brilliant deal in acquiring a company for us, I knew it would not be long before the acquired company realised that they had been short-changed. If that were to happen, then the five year growth I had hoped for from that company would be much more difficult to achieve. If the company felt good about the sale, then a positive result was much more likely.

Hence my brief to our financial people: if everybody leaves with a balloon, the party will be long remembered.

MAKE SURE THAT DEALS ARE FAIR FOR BOTH PARTIES, TO AVOID LONG-TERM DISCORD

94 Never Get Beguiled by the Process

There was a time when as a public company we were expanding our group. I was told that a very good company in our sphere of operations had fallen on hard times and was available for sale. After spending some time with the management, I became very interested in them as a candidate for acquisition by AMV.

There were 10 subsidiary companies operating under the holding company that I was in talks with. The process of interviewing everybody, as well as the due diligence required, took weeks and it became overwhelming. We finally got to midnight on the day that we were supposed to be signing the purchase agreement and every one of our conference rooms was full of people with their advisers.

As discussions went on I finally had a chance to sit and reflect on where we were. I realised that the goalposts had moved and we were a long way away from buying the company that offered the opportunity I saw in the first place. In the time since talks began, we had allowed the deal that we thought we were doing to be diluted by all sorts of things.

Just in time I understood that we had become immersed in the process and not the end result. I called off the proposed deal that evening. Some people were upset with me, especially those who had already started to emotionally spend the money they thought they were going to receive, but I knew I was being sensible so it was OK.

The closest analogy I can think of was during my early days in advertising when one of my great friends met and fell in love with a woman who was due to get married three months later to somebody else. She felt the same about him but the wedding machine had taken over. It ground on until the morning of the wedding. Guests from out of town had arrived, presents were being given, everyone was getting ready. But in the nick of time she had the courage to tell her father she couldn't go through with it because she had met someone else. Just as in my case, she was not popular for calling off 'the deal' but we were both right – it wouldn't have worked out in the long term.

DON'T LET PROCESS, THE THRILL OF THE CHASE, CLOUD YOUR JUDGEMENT

95 How Can You Tell If a Company is in Trouble?

Analysts in the City used to say that they wouldn't invest in companies that had a fountain in reception and a company helicopter. I'm sure that's a sensible tactic but I think there's a much simpler illustration of the cultural health of an organisation.

At one stage in my Millwall negotiations to try and stem the inexorable slide towards administration, I had an appointment to see the chief executive of a very, very large bank. He had his own private office in the giant granite building where his company had their headquarters.

I arrived rather early for my appointment and casually started reading some magazines that were scattered around in the reception area. One was an issue of *Newsweek* and I was horrified to read about an outbreak of hostilities in the Middle East. I thought that that particular confrontation had ended but here I was reading about it again. It was early in October and it was only when I turned to the magazine's front cover that I discovered it was dated June. The conflict I was reading about had happened three months earlier and the problems had been resolved by late September.

I thought it said an enormous amount about a company that should have valued relevance and precision above most things that nobody cared enough to keep the magazines in reception up to date.

Even small manifestations of carelessness give warning signals about a company's health. Not enough people had enough pride to make sure that the little things were attended to. In due course the bank was swallowed up by a competitor.

LACK OF ATTENTION TO SMALL DETAILS CAN ILLUSTRATE A LOT ABOUT LARGE COMPANIES

Once Abbott Mead Vickers became a public company, we had to decide how we would go forward. We believed we had a culture and a way of operating which would be attractive across a number of communication disciplines, so we decided to build a group. We started, however, by setting out what Abbott Mead Vickers the public company should be.

We defined it as a greenhouse into which we would put fledgling companies and allow them to blossom in the warmth of the Abbott Mead Vickers brand and culture. Once they had done that, we would encourage them to become little greenhouses of their own, retain their entrepreneurial spirit and use their greenhouse to grow other fledgling companies. We decided above all that we would not extinguish the entrepreneurial spirit present in the companies we acquired.

Every acquisition had to be carefully thought out. It usually began with a call to me from somebody saying they had never thought about selling their company, but they had had an approach and were now thinking about capitalising on their efforts. Having had a discussion, they would decide that the only company they wanted to sell their business to was Abbott Mead Vickers, or latterly Omnicom. I usually agreed to meet with them over breakfast for initial discussions. I did this deliber-ately to watch how they treated the waiters. While they could be really sycophantic to me, a clicking of fingers or an inability to say thank you to the staff demonstrated that they weren't the people for us.

If they passed the breakfast test, the next step would be to decide whether they were the best of breed, whether they were people we liked and whether there appeared to be a chemical attraction between our companies. We checked this out very carefully then finally had a dinner with all the significant players from their business and ours. We would sit around a table for a few hours to check that critical chemistry. If that test was passed, we would then begin the process of buying the company.

ONLY ACQUIRE THE BEST OF BREED AND MAKE SURE THAT YOUR COMPANY CULTURES ARE COMPATIBLE

AN OPPORTUNITY PRESENTS ITSELF

Early in 1979 a major player in American advertising, Ed McCabe of Scali, McCabe, Sloves (SMS), came to London to deliver a lecture at the IPA. He was the youngest copywriter ever to be inducted into the American Copywriting Hall of Fame and one of his main claims to that fame was his work on Volvo. David and Ron at that stage had produced some award-winning work in the press and on posters for the brand here in the UK. David knew Ed slightly so we arranged to have dinner while he was in town. David had a worldwide reputation and he, Ed and I got along famously.

SMS had recently been acquired by the worldwide Ogilvy Group and had been charged with developing an alternative 'global network with creativity at its heart'. SMS would own those agencies and in turn Ogilvy would own SMS. Ed talked to us over dinner about the possibilities of us joining this network. Fallon in Minneapolis was already part of this growing group of agencies, as was the Martin agency in Richmond, Virginia. Both were doing great work and we were intrigued. However, we'd only been going for 18 months and we were gaining traction quite quickly in the UK advertising market, so we felt it was far too early to sell a part of our business. Ed reported back to his boss Marvin Sloves that we were absolutely the sort of partners they should have in the UK.

Marvin, being the master of grand gestures, sent two Concorde return tickets to New York for David and me. It was irresistible. We flew over a week or so later and met with Marvin, Ed and their partners over dinner at the Four Seasons in New York. The stylish Sloves had his own table in the beautiful Pool Room, designed by Mies van der Rohe, in the Seagram Building on Park Avenue.

Marvin was a man of great style who reminded me immediately of Orson Welles (before the great director swelled up like a barrage balloon) in his style and voice. I also loved his quote when he sold his agency to Ogilvy. He was asked what the main difference was between SMS before the Ogilvy sale and after it. He replied that before the sale the partners did not have a pot to pee in but after they had spent the money from the sale they would have 26 bathrooms between them.

At the dinner he and Ed argued persuasively that because both AMV and SMS worked on Volvo and creativity was at the heart of both our offerings, they would be the ideal parents for us. They said it was inevitable that we would finish up with American partners one day and there would be nobody who we'd like to be more involved with than them. They were right, of course and so we agreed to become part of Ogilvy's global network.

There was an immediate bonding and the start of lifelong friendships – both Marvin and one of his partners, Alan Pesky, became godfathers to two of my sons and David and Eve often went on holiday with Joan and Sam Scali. David and I both loved the mercurial McCabe. During the negotiations, at an evening out at the Ritz Casino in London's Piccadilly, we really bonded as a trio when Ed disconcerted the rather po-faced staff by demanding they acquire a craps table for him so that he could have a proper gamble. The slightly surreal nature of the evening was compounded by David and me giving Ed a lift back to his hotel. The problem was that David had a Porsche 911 with virtually no passenger space at all and so Ed was jammed in the back doing a passable imitation of Harry Houdini. But from somewhere his right hand appeared – we both shook it and the deal was really on its way.

Despite our misgivings at selling too soon, the benefits of a relationship with this powerhouse New York operation were massively appealing. From the beginning, I spent a lot of time with Alan Pesky, who was one of the co-founders. We got along really well and he was the most benign of majority equity owning supervisors. He was always tanned and always looked superbly fit and indeed did work out daily. His wife, Wendy, was a member of a family who were very big in the perfume business. The fact that the deal was meant to be was reinforced by my wife's favourite perfume at the time being Oscar de la Renta, one of Wendy's father's biggest selling lines. Alan was a great boss and is still a great friend. So we did the deal which would remain in place for 10 years and only came to an end due to circumstances beyond our control. We all got along really well and grew together.

97 The Perils of Expansion – Don't Get Carried Away

In my early career I worked for a really good company called KMP. The partners created and built a very powerful business that was very successful in a short space of time. Without allowing the company time to mature in its marketplace, they got a bit carried away and started to believe that they were masters of their own particular universe. One day one of their UK clients, who was very happy with the work they were doing for them in their home market, suggested that their US business could be up for grabs if the partners opened a New York office. This was a very beguiling thought. KMP reasoned it couldn't be all that difficult to replicate their UK success in another market.

They soon found out how difficult it was when, after deploying some of their very valuable UK talent and a considerable amount of money, they had to close their fledgling New York office after less than two years. They believed their own publicity that if their methods worked in the UK they would surely work in the US – an incredibly dangerous assumption.

The resulting loss was over £1 million and because this happened nearly 40 years ago, today that would be a hit of more than 10 times as much, which is a lot of money.

ALWAYS EXAMINE THE POTENTIAL PITFALLS OF RAPID EXPANSION AS WELL AS THE EXPECTED REWARDS

98 How Does Becoming a Public Company Affect the Organisation?

I have always found it rather strange that a company that builds itself by behaving in a certain way throughout its formative years suddenly feels it has to change once it becomes a publicly quoted stock. The disciplines required to be a successful public company in terms of financial management, operating procedures, ability to grow and competitiveness within its marketplace remain exactly the same as they were before the IPO. Obviously there are prescribed governance requirements but those, in my experience, are not very onerous if the company was already managed properly. So if the company was well-run and successful before going public then the City will just want more of the same, which will include a clear strategy going forward and consistent financial performance.

We took the view that we should treat the City the same way as we behaved towards our biggest clients. That meant we should develop a relationship with our major shareholders, give them no unpleasant surprises, make sure that they were fully informed and talk to them often. Financial institutions have money to invest. Indeed, they need to invest. And so companies who perform well are much sought after by institutions which have large portfolios of companies in their investment vehicles. For a fund to be able to be confident in any of their investments is an enormous relief. We found that telling the truth works really well in the City, particularly if related to a reasonable performance.

At the end of our first year as a public company, I went up to Scotland to visit a potential investor, one of the giant Scottish insurance companies. This was my second visit following a series of trips to Glasgow and Edinburgh I did after the public launch. On arriving at this particular institution, I discovered that the fund manager I'd spoken to 12 months before had left. His successor informed me that his predecessor had left a note on the file saying, 'Mead seems to care more for the welfare of his staff than his shareholders'. He asked me to comment on this.

I replied that it was an absurd distinction but, if forced, I would argue that the people who work for our agency have to be foremost in our thoughts but looking after the interests of our people also meant looking after our shareholders – if our staff perform well so will our share price. Two weeks later that institution bought a sizeable chunk of equity in our company.

HOLD FAST TO THE PRINCIPLES THAT MADE YOU SUCCESSFUL WHEN YOU BECOME A PUBLIC COMPANY

99 Sit Back and Let Others Do It

After we became a public company we had the ambition and the wherewithal to expand our offering to clients. The communication process with consumers is wide and diverse and we reckoned that we should be represented in all the main disciplines with only two provisos. The first was that the company we became associated with should be best of breed, and secondly, they should share our beliefs and principles, particularly in the area of how people should be treated.

Beyond that, the strategy we adopted was clear. We would expand vertically in the significant areas to increase our relevance to our client base. Areas we covered were in the fields of PR, media planning and buying, customer magazines, direct marketing and sales promotion amongst others.

Typically, we acquired companies set up and run by entrepreneurs and once we'd bought the companies it always seemed to me to make the most sense to take advantage of the entrepreneurial spirit that they possessed. So in every instance I urged the new members of our group to expand horizontally. They knew the best other operators in their area of expertise more clearly than I ever could. Giving them the mandate to acquire companies in their chosen field had the twin effect of giving us potential new areas of revenue but also allowing them to carry on in the mindset of entrepreneurs.

TRUST PARTNER COMPANIES TO MAXIMISE THEIR OWN TALENTS

NOT A BAD WAY TO DEFINE YOUR CAREER

There are many things that I have to be grateful to the great ad man David Kingsley for – particularly his lessons on how people should be treated.

Close to his desk he had a framed cartoon from *The New Yorker* magazine. It depicted two executive types having lunch. The caption underneath was one saying to the other, 'What I really want is to do my bit for mankind and get a piece of the action.'

As long as you go about it in the right way, there is absolutely no problem in aspiring to get 'a piece of the action'.

100 Don't Believe in Old Wives' Tales

One of the most commonly used is 'nice guys finish last'.

This is patently untrue and is normally used by unpleasant people as an excuse for their bad behaviour.

**YOU DON'T HAVE TO BE
A MONSTER TO SUCCEED**

Peter Mead is currently Chairman of Omnicom Europe, part of one of the biggest communication groups in the world with a market cap of $15 billion.

Having left school at 16 to work in the dispatch department at a large advertising agency, his career took off in 1977 when, with David Abbott and Adrian Vickers, he co-founded Abbott Mead Vickers (amvbbdo.com) – which *Campaign* magazine later described as 'arguably the most successful British advertising agency of all time'.

In addition to his advertising career he has been Chairman of a football club, sat on the board of the London Docklands Development Corporation and was a Vice Chairman of the NSPCC Full Stop Appeal. In all, during a long life in business, he has sat on the board of over 25 companies.

In 2013 he received a CBE for services to the creative industries.